NASCAR SPRINT CUP SERIES 2012

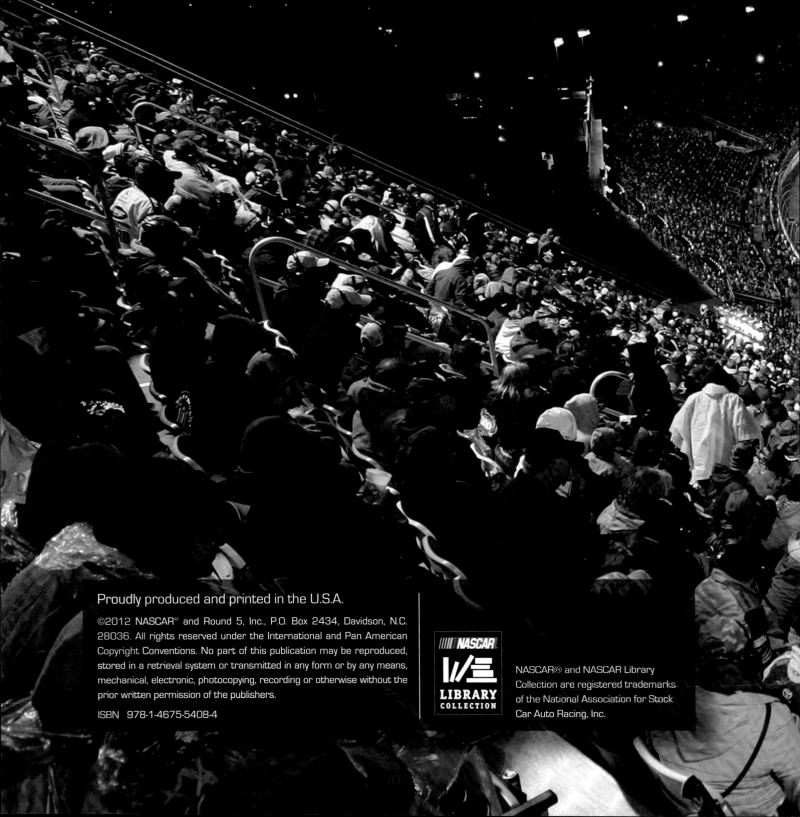

CONTENTS NASCAR SPRINT CUP SERIES 2012

//

//

ROUND 5 BOOKS   www.round5books.com

PUBLISHER	DIRECTOR OF CUSTOMER SERVICES	ART DIRECTION AND DESIGN
Bill Seaborn	Loren Seaborn	Randy Underwood

PHOTOGRAPHY	WRITER
CIA Stock Photography, Inc. ciastockphoto.com	Bob Zeller

PREFACE 2012

Above: From the drop of the green flag in the season-opening Daytona 500, the 2012 NASCAR Sprint Cup Series featured fierce competition, fender-slamming racing and nail-biting finishes, with 15 drivers visiting Victory Lane during the 36-race campaign.

Opposite page: On his way to his first NASCAR Sprint Cup Series championship, 28-year-old Brad Keselowski won five races in 2012, including the Food City 500 at Bristol Motor Speedway in March, his first win of the year.

The history of the NASCAR Sprint Cup Series is replete with championship battles where the points leader comes to the final race and suddenly finds himself in a new universe of racing, where simple challenges become difficult, and difficult ones become all but impossible.

As it was for Benny Parsons, who won the 1973 title with a wrecked car, and Jeff Gordon, who staggered to his first title with a 32nd-place finish in the last race of 1995, so to it was for Brad Keselowski. The 28-year-old Michigan native found himself in a whole different world as he fought and clawed and fell behind and ultimately triumphed in his first run for a championship. It was a trial by fire every bit as pressure packed as a seventh game of a World Series, or the back nine at the Masters.

"It's not easy to do when you come down here [to Homestead-Miami Speedway] and have everything on the line," said five-time champ Jimmie Johnson.

Keselowski had come to the Ford EcoBoost 400 at Homestead with a 20-point cushion in the Chase for the NASCAR Sprint Cup, needing only a 15th-place finish to win the title. It was enough of a margin to give some comfort, but not big enough to prevent him from being nervous. One bad break could easily spell doom for the driver of the Penske Racing No. 2 Miller Lite Dodge.

It was Johnson who put Keselowski in the pressure cooker at Homestead, technically taking the championship lead from Keselowski several times during the race as he executed a superb gas-saving strategy. Ironically, though, it was Johnson who ultimately cracked under the pressure. Leading with only 62 laps to go, Johnson came to the pits for his final stop

Above: Dale Earnhardt Jr. (No. 88), the nine-time Most Popular Driver of the Year in NASCAR, celebrated with his fans when he won his first race in four years at Michigan International Speedway in June.

Opposite page: The magic between driver Jimmie Johnson and crew chief Chad Knaus that helped lead to five straight NASCAR Sprint Cup Series championships was not quite effective enough to deliver a sixth title in 2012, but good enough for five race victories and third place in the Chase for the NASCAR Sprint Cup.

and met disaster. The rear tire changer didn't get a lug nut secured on the left rear wheel, forcing Johnson to pit again and sending him a lap down. Finally, the pressure was off for Keselowski. The championship was his.

Keselowski had been in deep trouble at the time, mired in 24th place. But suddenly, through the earpieces inside his full-face racing helmet, he heard his crew chief, Paul Wolfe, say, "I've got a big picture story if you want to hear it. The car in front of you (Johnson) has a penalty. The car in front of you will be pitting again."

When Johnson's car broke about 20 laps later and left the race, it meant only that he would lose second place in the final points standings to Clint Bowyer, who finished second in the race.

By winning the NASCAR Sprint Cup championship in only his third full season, Keselowski reached NASCAR's pinnacle faster than every other champion except two in the modern NASCAR era, which began in 1972. Dale Earnhardt won in his second full season in 1980, and Gordon, like Keselowski, was in his third full season in the final race of 1995.

"It feels pretty good. It feels really good," Keselowski said. "I can't believe how everything just came together over the last what's it been, three years? And you know what? I feel like the best is yet to come. I really do." Keselowski's first championship was also the first NASCAR Sprint Cup car owner's championship for a legend in American motorsports, Roger Penske.

In the crucible of the season's final race, it's easy to overlook that it was all set up by a long season of other contests, each adding incrementally to each driver's record and gradually separating them, so by year's end, the ultimate champion is fairly and conclusively identified.

Although the Chase for the NASCAR Sprint Cup came down to two drivers in the final race, it was a wide-open contest throughout the long season, especially among the manufacturers. Each of NASCAR's four manufacturers – Ford, Chevy, Dodge and Toyota – won one of the season's first four races.

When Matt Kenseth roared across the finish line first in the Daytona 500, it was his second win in the Great American Race in four years and Ford's second victory in a row. The race also featured the most spectacular incident of the season when Juan Pablo Montoya's rear end broke as he was zipping around the track and his car spun into the truck carrying the jet dryer, breaking open the jet fuel tank and starting a fire. No one was hurt, but the race had to be stopped to extinguish the fire and make the track surface race-able.

A week after Daytona, Denny Hamlin steered his Toyota into Victory Lane in Phoenix. Seven days after that, it was Chevy's turn, with Tony Stewart taking the checkered flag at Las Vegas. And on March 18, less than a month into the season, all four manufacturers had tasted victory when Dodge driver Keselowski triumphed at Bristol in the first of his five race wins in 2012.

After only three months of racing in 2012, no fewer than nine drivers had driven their cars into Victory Lane at NASCAR Sprint Cup tracks. By the time the series reached Pocono in June, four drivers – Stewart, Hamlin, Keselowski and Johnson – had won two races and begun to set the standard that they would maintain throughout the season and into the Chase.

The Pocono 400, however, would bring yet another winner – the season's 10th – when Joey Logano finally broke through for his first victory since a rain-shortened win in 2009. And then came Michigan, and sweet victory, finally, for Dale Earnhardt Jr. and his fans. Earnhardt's win in the Quicken Loans 400 ended a four-year victory drought. The following week, on the road course at Sonoma, Clint Bowyer showed never-before-seen road-racing skills on his way to become the 12th different NASCAR Sprint Cup race winner only 16 races into the season.

In August, Jeff Gordon and Marco Ambrose became the 13th and 14th NASCAR Sprint Cup drivers to win in 2012, with Gordon happy to take a rain-shortened victory at Pocono and Ambrose showing off his road-racing talent in a wild last-lap battle with Keselowski at Watkins Glen.

And when it came to the Chase itself, the season's dominant drivers rose to the top, with Keselowski winning the first race at Chicago, Hamlin taking the second contest at New Hampshire, and Keselowski charging back to win at Dover and take charge of the Chase points lead.

Keselowski would not win another Chase race, but he would hang tough, eventually giving up the points lead to Johnson. But when Johnson blew a tire and smacked the wall at Phoenix in the second-to-last race, Keselowski was back in front in the Chase, with only one more mountain to climb. And as he learned, it was as daunting as climbing Mt. Everest.

NASCAR Sprint Cup Series Champion
BRAD KESELOWSKI

Above: Youth triumphs again as 28-year-old Brad Keselowski burns yellow-tinged rubber at Homestead-Miami Speedway.

Opposite page: Keselowski hoists the NASCAR Sprint Cup Series trophy after winning his first championship in NASCAR's premier series.

In 2008, a youthful Michigan driver who looked even younger than his 24 years crawled behind the wheel of a Hendrick Motorsports Chevrolet to qualify for his first NASCAR Sprint Cup Series race at Charlotte Motor Speedway.

His name was Brad Keselowski, and anyone familiar with Midwestern short-track racing was familiar with the name Keselowski. His grandfather, "Papa" John Keselowski, began racing in the 1950s, and his father, Bob, and uncle, Ron, picked up the sport and carried on the family tradition through the rest of the 20th century. Bob eventually passed the family tradition on to his two eager sons, Brad and Brian.

But the family name carried little weight and no magic that day at Charlotte. Brad Keselowski failed to qualify for the race. He did make his first two NASCAR Sprint Cup starts later that season in the same car, but at Speedweeks in February 2009, behind the wheel of a James Finch-owned Chevy, Keselowski failed to make his first Daytona 500. It was not the most encouraging start for a driver destined to charge to his first NASCAR Sprint Cup championship in only his third full season in the series.

"Well, it's been a long road from where I started to where I'm at now," Keselowski said on the eve of his first championship "I did not start out right here," he said, holding his hand high. "I started out way down here, and my success story is attributed to a constant desire to improve, and that's how I've got to where I'm at, and that's how I feel like I'll continue to be successful—a commitment to improvement every day. I want to be better tomorrow than I was today and better in the future than I was tomorrow."

Above: The third-generation Michigan driver exuded confidence and determination throughout the 2012 season.

Opposite page top: His crew high-fived each other on pit road and then celebrated with their driver in Victory Lane.

Opposite page bottom: Keselowski scored the first of his five victories of the 2012 season at Bristol Motor Speedway in March.

Though Keselowski failed to qualify for the 2009 Daytona 500, it was at the very next superspeedway race, at Talladega Superspeedway, where he served notice that he was a force to be reckoned with on the race track. Driving Finch's Chevy again, and competing for a car owner who had never won a NASCAR Sprint Cup race in almost 20 years of trying, Keselowski won the race after leading only that wild final lap that saw Carl Edwards' Ford fly into the catch fence.

He had won his first NASCAR Sprint Cup race in only his fifth start, and he followed that up with two more top-10 finishes in his next two starts. Later that year, Roger Penske signed him to run a full season in 2010. And after he finished eighth for Finch in the second race at Talladega, Penske put him behind the wheel of one of his Dodges the following week at Texas.

Fortunately for Keselowski, the veteran car owner has a level of patience honed over a lifetime of the ups and downs of racing. Penske did not panic when his new young driver finished 35th, 37th and 25th in his first three races. And he did not flinch the following year, despite fielding Keselowski's car largely without sponsorship, when his young phenom flopped, posting only two top 10s, both 10th-place finishes, and not getting those until the season was almost over. Keselowski was certainly aggressive, but he wasn't getting the results.

"Early on there, he was rough, he was bumping people," said Penske. "But I think that he's emerged. He's learned, like a lot of the great drivers that have gone through that rough patch. He's emerged, and I think to me, the speed that he's come from where he was when he first started with us to where he is today—smooth, understanding the car, and ultimately being a winner—to me is amazing. He's done it in just 36 months with us."

In 2011, Paul Wolfe became Keselowski's crew chief and that elusive bonding agent known colloquially as "chemistry" blossomed in the new relationship. "When Brad and I first got together, part of the reason I was excited about working with Brad is because I had seen him win races in cars that I thought weren't as good as maybe cars I was putting on the race track at the time," Wolfe said. "As a crew chief or a team, that's always what you want, you want a guy that you know can win races when you might not have the best race car out there."

"I feel so lucky to have him," said Keselowski. "Some drivers go their whole career and never have a crew chief like him."

Keselowski won three races in 2011 and finished a strong fifth in the Chase for the NASCAR Sprint Cup, all the while becoming more of a leader at Penske Racing as he gained experience. With the departure of Kurt Busch from the team at the end of 2011, "I sat down with Brad and said, 'You're going to have to be the leader of this team,'" Penske said. "Once Kurt left and he stepped into the leadership position, he's just taken it over."

Keselowski began pushing and challenging a car owner well-known for already demanding the utmost of his teams and drivers. "I'd have to say that Brad has not only pushed me as an individual, he's pushed the team in a positive direction, and he's delivering. It's one thing when someone is pushing you and they don't deliver, but he seems to be able to give us that extra push but (also) deliver on the race weekends. . ."

The young driver unquestionably wanted a championship to fulfill his own deeply held ambitions, but he also wanted it for the legendary car owner who, at 75, was old enough to be his grandfather, but had not yet won a NASCAR Sprint Cup car owner's championship.

In 1972, more than a decade before Keselowski was even born, Penske had fielded his car as a NASCAR owner, putting Mark Donohue in an AMC Matador at the road course at Riverside. In the 29 seasons he's been active in NASCAR, Penske's cars have started nearly 1,400 races, winning 73 of them. Penske finished second in the championship with Rusty Wallace

Above: Keselowski's crew peels off a fast pit stop at Texas Motor Speedway in November, helping him on his way to a runner-up finish

Right: Keselowski and crew chief Paul Wolfe hoist the NASCAR Sprint Cup champion's trophy at Homestead-Miami Speedway.

Opposite page bottom: The king of NASCAR in 2012 was also the king of social media in the NASCAR Sprint Cup Series.

in 1993, but has fared no better than third in any other season-long campaign. It was a yawning gap in the car owner's otherwise success-studded racing record.

Keselowski's personal ambition became supercharged by the desire to deliver that elusive crown to his car owner. What do you give a billionaire that he can't buy himself? How about a championship in NASCAR's most elite series? "That's what drives me—to be the guy to win the first championship for him," Keselowski said

before the race at Homestead. "I want to be that guy."

And so he was. As far as his own record, Keselowski joined Dale Earnhardt and Jeff Gordon to become only the third driver in NASCAR's modern era, dating back to 1972, to win a NASCAR Sprint Cup championship in three full seasons or less.

"It's been such a ride," Keselowski said. "And every bump along the way has made it that much sweeter."

 01

Daytona International Speedway
Monday, February 27, 2012

DAYTONA 500

It took a steady hand to navigate the 2012 Daytona 500, with its relentless rains and its trial by fire, so it was not surprising that first under the checkered flag in what became an endurance race was Matt Kenseth, one of the most patient, even-tempered, least demonstrative drivers in the NASCAR Sprint Cup Series.

Richard Petty said some years ago that he thought Kenseth was the driver most like him in the series because of his ability to stick around, often in the shadows, and then be able to take advantage at the end.

And that's exactly what Kenseth did, although in this race, "sticking around" not only meant waiting a day and a half, but overcoming a variety of problems with the No. 17 Best Buy Ford. Kenseth did not lead the Daytona 500 until lap 146, but from there he was in front for 50 of the final 57 laps, including the last 38 laps, beating Dale Earnhardt Jr. to the finish line by 0.21 of a second in a green-white-checkered overtime finish. Greg Biffle, who started on the outside of the first row, finished third after leading 44 laps, followed by Denny Hamlin and Jeff Burton.

"We had a really fast car all day, (but) had a lot of adversity to overcome, a lot of problems with the car. We were able to get it figured out and had a great pit stop at the end that put us in position, and it feels great," Kenseth said in the winner's interview. "I wasn't expecting to win when I woke up this morning, so it feels good to be sitting here," he added in his typically understated manner.

It was Kenseth's second Daytona 500 victory (he also won in 2009) and, coupled with his 2003 championship, further enhances his Hall of Fame-level record as one of the premier drivers of his time.

Although the fans were graced with several days of

The 43-car field streaks under the green flag to begin an unprecedented Monday night, prime-time running of the Daytona 500.

Florida-pure sunshine leading up to the Daytona 500, on race day itself, passing showers washed out the show, and the rain continued until Monday afternoon, finally giving NASCAR its first chance on Monday evening. It was a bad break that was so bad, it finally went to good, because the race aired in prime time, like the championship game of the NCAA Final Four or a Monday night NFL football game.

The drivers took advantage of the opportunity by immediately pressing the action button. At the beginning of the second lap, as the pack roared toward the first turn, Elliott Sadler got into the back of Jimmie Johnson, sending Johnson into the outside wall and triggering a five-car crash that also collected Danica Patrick, who was competing in her first NASCAR Sprint Cup race. After that, the race settled down, with Biffle and Hamlin leading most of the time, and only minor incidents interrupting the action.

Kenseth was hanging around near the front, but was preoccupied with irritations. "We had a lot of problems and almost ended up a lap down," he said in Victory Lane. "I had my radio break and my tach break and we pushed all the water out and had to come in and put water in it. These (crew) guys did a great job. They never panicked and I think they enjoyed their day more because they couldn't hear me on the radio with my radio problems."

On lap 157, David Stremme spun in turn three and brought out the yellow flag for the seventh time. It was a minor thing and the caution period was as routine as could be until lap 160. Juan Pablo Montoya was barreling down the backstretch at high speed to catch up with the field before the restart when a truck arm broke on his suspension and sent the car into a spin. Sideways,

Right: Trevor Bayne, winner of the 2011 Daytona 500, works on his car during practice for the NASCAR Nationwide Series race.

Below: Danica Patrick is deep in thought during practice for the Gatorade Duel qualifying races before the Daytona 500 at Daytona International Speedway.

Above: Kyle Busch somehow did not wreck after this wild sideways ride in the Budweiser Shootout during 2012 Speedweeks at Daytona International Speedway.

Left: Wearing the T-shirt of one of his sponsors, Dale Earnhardt Jr. strides through the pits at Daytona International Speedway.

Following spread: Tony Stewart in the No. 14 Office Depot/Mobil 1 Chevrolet and Ricky Stenhouse Jr. (No. 6), tangle at the start-finish line with three laps to go, triggering an eight-car crash and prompting a green-white-checkered overtime finish.

Montoya's Chevrolet slammed into the whining engine of the jet dryer truck that was up against the wall at the entrance of turn three. A big explosion was followed by an even bigger fire as the 200 gallons of jet kerosene on the truck began pouring down the banking of the track.

Shaken but unhurt, Montoya staggered from his car, which was burning front and rear. "I've hit a lot of things - but a jet dryer?" he said afterwards. "As I was talking on the radio, the car just turned right."

The race was red-flagged for the next two hours and five minutes as fire fighters put out the fire and track crews began the painstaking process of scrubbing the track (using Tide detergent, of course) and making sure it was ready for racing. In the meantime, the drivers crawled out of their cars on the backstretch to mill around, some gathering to watch Brad Keselowski tweet

about the ongoing situation on his mobile phone to a legion of Twitter followers that grew exponentially with each new message. "You would think after 65 years and running all the races that NASCAR has run that you've seen about everything.....," said NASCAR President Mike Helton.

Kenseth grabbed the lead with a quick stop during the round of pit stops that occurred just before the green flag fell again, and he led the rest of the way, avoiding all the trouble involved in three late-race, multi-car accidents and fending off all challengers on the restarts, including the final two-lap overtime laps 201 and 202.

"It's nice to go the whole distance and survive a green white-checkered, too, because you just don't know what's going to happen in speed races," Kenseth said. Indeed.

01 | Daytona 500

FIN	ST	CAR	DRIVER	SPONSOR	LAPS
1	4	17	Matt Kenseth	Best Buy Ford	202
2	5	88	Dale Earnhardt Jr	Diet Mountain Dew/National Guard Chevrolet	202
3	2	16	Greg Biffle	3M Ford	202
4	31	11	Denny Hamlin	FedEx Express Toyota	202
5	9	31	Jeff Burton	Caterpillar Chevrolet	202
6	37	27	Paul Menard	Menards/Peak Chevrolet	202
7	13	29	Kevin Harvick	Budweiser Chevrolet	202
8	1	99	Carl Edwards	Fastenal Ford	202
9	12	20	Joey Logano	The Home Depot Toyota	202
10	22	55	Mark Martin	Aaron's Toyota	202
11	30	15	Clint Bowyer	5-hour Energy Toyota	202
12	26	56	Martin Truex Jr	NAPA Auto Parts Toyota	202
13	7	9	Marcos Ambrose	Stanley Ford	202
14	32	47	Bobby Labonte	Kroger Toyota	202
15	24	36	Dave Blaney	Ollie's Bargain Outlet Chevrolet	202
16	3	14	Tony Stewart	Office Depot/Mobil 1 Chevrolet	202
17	14	18	Kyle Busch	M&M's Brown Toyota	202
18	43	32	Terry Labonte	C&J Energy Ford	202
19	41	26	Tony Raines	Front Row Motorsports Ford	202
20	21	6	Ricky Stenhouse Jr	Ford EcoBoost Ford	202
21	18	39	Ryan Newman	U.S. ARMY/Quicken Loans Chevrolet	202
22	39	83	Landon Cassill	Burger King Toyota	202
23	33	38	David Gilliland	MHP/Power Pak Pudding Ford	201
24	6	78	Regan Smith	Furniture Row/CSX Play It Safe Chevrolet	200
25	36	13	Casey Mears	GEICO Ford	199
26	38	93	David Reutimann	Burger King Toyota	196
27	10	33	Elliott Sadler	General Mills/Kroger Chevrolet	196
28	34	87	Joe Nemechek	AM FM Energy Wood & Pellet Stoves Toyota	194
29	20	5	Kasey Kahne	Farmers Insurance Chevrolet	189
30	11	98	Michael McDowell	KLOVE/Curb Records Ford	189
31	19	1	Jamie McMurray	Bass Pro Shops/Tracker Boats Chevrolet	188
32	23	2	Brad Keselowski	Miller Lite Dodge	187
33	27	43	Aric Almirola	Smithfield Helping Hungry Homes Ford	187
34	15	22	AJ Allmendinger	Shell Pennzoil Dodge	177
35	40	21	Trevor Bayne	Motorcraft/Quick Lane Tire & Auto Center Ford	164
36	35	42	Juan Pablo Montoya	Target Chevrolet	159
37	42	30	David Stremme	Inception Motorsports Toyota	156
38	29	10	Danica Patrick	GoDaddy.com Chevrolet	138
39	28	51	Kurt Busch	Hendrickcars.com Chevrolet	113
40	16	24	Jeff Gordon	Drive to End Hunger Chevrolet	81
41	17	7	Robby Gordon	MAPEI/Menards/SPEED Energy Dodge	25
42	8	48	Jimmie Johnson	Lowe's Chevrolet	1
43	25	34	David Ragan	Scorpion Truck Bedliners Ford	1

*Sunoco Rookie of the Year Contender

NASCAR Sprint Cup Series TOP 12
(After 1 Race)

Pos.	Driver	Points	Pos.	Driver	Points
1	MATT KENSETH	47	7	KEVIN HARVICK	37
2	DALE EARNHARDT JR	42	8	CARL EDWARDS	36
3	GREG BIFFLE	42	9	JOEY LOGANO	36
4	DENNY HAMLIN	42	10	MARK MARTIN	35
5	JEFF BURTON	40	11	CLINT BOWYER	33
6	PAUL MENARD	39	12	MARTIN TRUEX JR	33

Opposite page: Matt Kenseth (No. 17) leads the field under the green flag during a late-race restart in the Daytona 500, moments before (Above) hoisting the Harley Earl Trophy in Victory Lane after winning his second Daytona 500.

02

SUBWAY FRESH FIT 500

As the long campaign for the NASCAR Sprint Cup Series gets underway in earnest every February, one of the best ways for a driver to set himself up for a good year is to win early. And after a disappointing 2011 season following his near-championship run in 2010, Denny Hamlin made a statement about his 2012 intentions by coming on strong at the end to score a convincing win in the SUBWAY Fresh Fit 500 at Phoenix International Raceway.

Hamlin, surprising himself with the victory, led the final 59 laps in his No. 11 FedEx Office Toyota on his way to a comfortable 7.315-second win over Kevin Harvick. Greg Biffle scored his second straight third-place finish, followed by Jimmie Johnson and Brad Keselowski.

The finish was becoming a nail-biter as Harvick relentlessly moved closer to Hamlin's rear bumper in the final laps while both drivers worried about low fuel. But with three laps to go on the one-mile oval, Harvick's engine sputtered and the challenge was over. Harvick still managed to hang on to second while Hamlin scooted over the finish line with his eight cylinders still getting the fuel they needed.

Hamlin started 13th on a sunny and warm day, but he only led two laps before his final run to the flag. He beat Harvick on a restart with 59 laps left and survived one more restart on his way to Victory Lane.

"I don't know where this came from," Hamlin said in the winner's interview. "I don't know how our car was as good as it was today. We were solidly off in practice. We were off, but we kept getting it better and closer to being competitive. But I had no idea we were going to fire off like we did today. You know, it just seemed like we kept improving our car...."

It's the crew chief who orders the adjustments to improve the car, and so the victory was particularly satisfying for

Opting to start on the outside, Denny Hamlin (No. 11) leads the field at a restart in the SUBWAY Fresh Fit 500, with Brad Keselowski (No. 2) to his inside.

Above: Kevin Harvick makes a pit stop in his No. 29 Rheem Chevrolet at Phoenix International Raceway.

Opposite Page: Autograph-hungry fans tag along with Carl Edwards as he walks through the garage area at Phoenix International Raceway.

Darian Grubb, who became Hamlin's crew chief after being released by Tony Stewart after winning the NASCAR Sprint Cup championship with him. The low-key Grubb handled the dismissal with class and quiet dignity, but to win almost right out of the box with his new driver was special.

"I guess you could say it is a little bit of vindication, but I really don't think that way," Grubb said. "I try to just think the high road all the time. I feel like I came into a very good situation."

The Phoenix track had left Hamlin with bad memories in 2010 when, while leading the Chase for the NASCAR Sprint Cup, he was forced to pit late in the race for fuel and dropped to a 19th-place finish, allowing Jimmie Johnson to close the gap in what became his fifth straight NASCAR Sprint Cup title.

But following the disappointment of 2011, when he won only a single race and failed to contend during the Chase, Hamlin picked the Phoenix area to escape from it all, renting a house in Paradise Valley for almost two months during the off season, using the dry, warm desert air to clear his head.

"I mean, last year, we just never got going," Hamlin said. "Yeah, maybe there was a hangover effect for the first half of the year. You can claim that. But it didn't have anything to do with how bad I ran the last 10 races. We just didn't have it all together. But we've made some good changes within our organization."

02 | SUBWAY Fresh Fit 500

FIN	ST	CAR	DRIVER	SPONSOR	LAPS
1	13	11	Denny Hamlin	FedEx Office Toyota	312
2	8	29	Kevin Harvick	Rheem Chevrolet	312
3	7	16	Greg Biffle	3MWraps.com Ford	312
4	4	48	Jimmie Johnson	Lowe's / Kobalt Tools Chevrolet	312
5	28	2	Brad Keselowski	Miller Lite Dodge	312
6	12	18	Kyle Busch	M&M's Brown Toyota	312
7	25	56	Martin Truex Jr	NAPA Filters Toyota	312
8	30	24	Jeff Gordon	Drive to End Hunger Chevrolet	312
9	1	55	Mark Martin	Aaron's Toyota	312
10	9	20	Joey Logano	The Home Depot Toyota	312
11	5	42	Juan Pablo Montoya	Target Chevrolet	312
12	18	43	Aric Almirola	Smithfield / Allez Cuisine Ford	312
13	26	17	Matt Kenseth	Best Buy Ford	312
14	29	88	Dale Earnhardt Jr	National Guard / Diet Mountain Dew Chevrolet	312
15	19	51	Kurt Busch	Phoenix Construction Services Chevrolet	312
16	17	47	Bobby Labonte	Kingsford / Scotts Toyota	312
17	24	99	Carl Edwards	SUBWAY Ford	312
18	15	22	AJ Allmendinger	Shell Pennzoil Dodge	311
19	41	93	Travis Kvapil	Burger King / Dr. Pepper Toyota	311
20	3	78	Regan Smith	Furniture Row Racing / Farm American Chevrolet	311
21	6	39	Ryan Newman	WIX Filters Chevrolet	310
22	2	14	Tony Stewart	Office Depot / Mobil 1 Chevrolet	310
23	23	36	Dave Blaney	Ollie's Bargain Outlet Chevrolet	309
24	42	32	Mike Bliss	Southern Pride Trucking / U.S. Chrome Ford	309
25	34	34	David Ragan	Barrett-Jackson Ford	309
26	35	49	J.J. Yeley	America Israel Racing Toyota	309
27	40	33	Brendan Gaughan	South Point Hotel & Casino Chevrolet	308
28	36	38	David Gilliland	Rick Santorum for President Ford	308
29	43	30	David Stremme	Inception Motorsports Toyota	306
30	16	15	Clint Bowyer	5-hour Energy Toyota	306
31	20	27	Paul Menard	Menards / Tarkett Chevrolet	303
32	14	9	Marcos Ambrose	Stanley Ford	295
33	11	31	Jeff Burton	Wheaties Chevrolet	291
34	10	5	Kasey Kahne	Farmers Insurance Chevrolet	274
35	22	83	Landon Cassill	Burger King / Dr. Pepper Toyota	272
36	32	10	David Reutimann	Accell Construction Chevrolet	248
37	21	1	Jamie McMurray	Bass Pro Shops / Tracker Boats Chevrolet	212
38	33	26	Josh Wise *	Morristown Drivers Service Ford	110
39	31	13	Casey Mears	GEICO Ford	109
40	38	87	Joe Nemechek	AM/FM Energy Wood & Pellet Stoves Toyota	62
41	39	7	Robby Gordon	SPEED Energy / Bashas' Dodge	33
42	27	23	Scott Riggs	North Texas Pipe Chevrolet	29
43	37	98	Michael McDowell	Curb Records Ford	8

*Sunoco Rookie of the Year Contender

NASCAR Sprint Cup Series
TOP 12
(After 2 Races)

Pos.	Driver	Points	Pos.	Driver	Points
1	DENNY HAMLIN	89	7	MARK MARTIN	71
2	GREG BIFFLE	83	8	JOEY LOGANO	70
3	KEVIN HARVICK	81	9	KYLE BUSCH	66
4	MATT KENSETH	79	10	CARL EDWARDS	63
5	DALE EARNHARDT JR.	72	11	BOBBY LABONTE	58
6	MARTIN TRUEX JR.	71	12	BRAD KESELOWSKI	52

Above: Denny Hamlin's trip to Victory Lane at Phoenix was his first at the one-mile oval.

Opposite page: (Top left) A tire specialist works his magic in the pits at Phoenix while (Top right) the No. 78 Furniture Row Racing/Farm American Chevrolet driven by Regan Smith, flanked by Kasey Kahne (No. 5), leads the field before a restart at Phoenix after (Bottom) successfully navigating NASCAR pre-race inspection.

03

Las Vegas Motor Speedway
Sunday, March 11, 2012

KOBALT TOOLS 400

While Las Vegas Motor Speedway didn't exactly owe Tony Stewart a win in the Kobalt Tools 400 at Las Vegas Motor Speedway, the NASCAR Sprint Cup Series champion took matters into his own hands and convincingly won the race that had eluded his grasp in 2011.

Tony Stewart dominated the 2011 running of the race, but a pit road penalty forced his team to play catch up and ultimately was enough to make the difference between winning and finishing second behind Carl Edwards.

This time around, Stewart didn't lead until the race was halfway over, taking over the top spot for the first time on lap 134 of the 267-lap contest. But from there, he led all but seven laps the rest of the way, finishing 0.461 of a second ahead of Jimmie Johnson. Greg Biffle scored his third consecutive third-place finish and was rewarded for his consistency with the points lead in the race to the Chase for the NASCAR Sprint Cup. Ryan Newman, Stewart's teammate, finished fourth, followed by Carl Edwards.

"Just an awesome day," Stewart said in the winner's interview. "We felt like after Happy Hour yesterday we had a really good, solid, fairly balanced race car. That's probably the best I felt leaving Happy Hour in a long time. But you knew it was going to be a tough day to get an advantage."

After Stewart got to the front, he had to survive five restarts after yellow flags, even through the race was largely trouble free. Three of the five caution periods were prompted by debris on the track, another was caused by fluid on the racing surface and the fifth was for a single-car incident.

"Every time the caution came out, you knew that was another heat cycle on the tires. Our car was so, so strong today on restarts. We could get to the start/finish line and get to turn one so good today, that was a big key in holding

Pole winner Kasey Kahne (No. 5) leads the 43-car field under the green flag to start the 2012 Kobalt Tools 400 at Las Vegas Motor Speedway

these guys off," Stewart said. "It seemed like we were a little bit weaker than the guys behind us for the first three laps. Then the next three laps, we would break even. After six or seven laps, we would start pulling away.

"It was a matter of getting a good restart, hitting our marks for a couple laps, (and) going on. Every time the caution came out, you cringed knowing you were giving them another opportunity to take a shot. Seemed like everybody got their turn at it – just a different person on each restart that we had to hold off."

It was the 45th career victory for the defending champion and three-time title winner, but the first with his new crew chief, Steve Addington. The win moves Stewart into 15th place all by himself on the all-time NASCAR winner's roster, just ahead of Bill Elliott with 44 wins. But perhaps more importantly, it keeps his momentum going after his remarkable run to the championship. He won five of the 10 Chase races last year, and with his victory at Las Vegas, Stewart claimed his sixth victory in 13 events, earning every bit of this one.

"That's what made today a little more special," he said. "It wasn't handed to us. Not only did we have to fight off a challenge once, we had to do it about four or five times in the last 30 laps. It makes you feel like you've earned your deal."

Above: Joey Logano spins out his right hand with his left hand while discussing on-track action with Brad Keselowski.

Opposite page: On his way to victory, Tony Stewart (No. 14) battles below Clint Bowyer (No. 15) going into the first turn at Phoenix, with Greg Biffle (No. 16) and Matt Kenseth (No.17) trailing.

03 | Kobalt Tools 400

FIN	ST	CAR	DRIVER	SPONSOR	LAPS
1	7	14	Tony Stewart	Mobil 1/Office Depot Chevrolet	267
2	6	48	Jimmie Johnson	Lowe's/Kobalt Tools Chevrolet	267
3	9	16	Greg Biffle	3M/Meguiars Ford	267
4	18	39	Ryan Newman	Quicken Loans Chevrolet	267
5	21	99	Carl Edwards	Aflac Ford	267
6	5	15	Clint Bowyer	5-hour Energy Toyota	267
7	26	27	Paul Menard	Menards/Schrock Chevrolet	267
8	19	1	Jamie McMurray	McDonald's Chevrolet	267
9	25	21	Trevor Bayne	Motorcraft/Quick Lane Tire & Auto Center Ford	267
10	4	88	Dale Earnhardt Jr	National Guard/Diet Mountain Dew Chevrolet	267
11	3	29	Kevin Harvick	Budweiser Chevrolet	267
12	16	24	Jeff Gordon	DuPont 20 Years Chevrolet	267
13	15	9	Marcos Ambrose	DeWalt Ford	267
14	22	31	Jeff Burton	Caterpillar Chevrolet	267
15	28	78	Regan Smith	Furniture Row/Farm American Chevrolet	267
16	8	20	Joey Logano	Dollar General Toyota	267
17	10	56	Martin Truex Jr	NAPA Auto Parts Toyota	267
18	13	55	Mark Martin	Aaron's Toyota	267
19	1	5	Kasey Kahne	Farmers Insurance Chevrolet	267
20	17	11	Denny Hamlin	FedEx Freight Toyota	267
21	35	34	David Ragan	Front Row Motorsports Ford	267
22	11	17	Matt Kenseth	Zest Ford	267
23	2	18	Kyle Busch	M&M's Brown Toyota	266
24	27	43	Aric Almirola	Richard Petty Fantasy Racing Camp Ford	266
25	29	42	Juan Pablo Montoya	Clorox Chevrolet	264
26	24	47	Bobby Labonte	Kingsford/Bush's Beans Toyota	264
27	32	13	Casey Mears	GEICO Ford	264
28	43	30	David Stremme	Inception Motorsports Toyota	263
29	38	36	Dave Blaney	Ollie's Bargain Outlet Chevrolet	263
30	41	32	Ken Schrader	Federated Auto Parts Ford	263
31	31	10	David Reutimann	Accell Construction Chevrolet	261
32	20	2	Brad Keselowski	Miller Lite Dodge	259
33	34	38	David Gilliland	Front Row Motorsports Ford	258
34	23	33	Brendan Gaughan	South Point Casino Chevrolet	252
35	12	51	Kurt Busch	Tag Heuer Eyewear Chevrolet	251
36	30	83	Landon Cassill	Burger King Toyota	240
37	14	22	AJ Allmendinger	Pennzoil Dodge	238
38	39	98	Michael McDowell	Phil Parsons Racing Ford	147
39	37	93	Travis Kvapil	Burger King Toyota	123
40	33	26	Josh Wise *	1-800-Loan Mart Ford	64
41	40	87	Joe Nemechek	AM FM Energy Wood & Pellet Stoves Toyota	44
42	42	37	Timmy Hill *	Poynt.com Ford	42
43	36	49	J.J. Yeley	America Israel Racing Toyota	39

*Sunoco Rookie of the Year Contender

NASCAR Sprint Cup Series TOP 12
(After 3 Races)

Pos.	Driver	Points	Pos.	Driver	Points
1	GREG BIFFLE	125	7	TONY STEWART	100
2	KEVIN HARVICK	115	8	MARTIN TRUEX JR.	98
3	DENNY HAMLIN	113	9	JOEY LOGANO	98
4	DALE EARNHARDT JR.	107	10	MARK MARTIN	97
5	MATT KENSETH	102	11	PAUL MENARD	89
6	CARL EDWARDS	102	12	KYLE BUSCH	87

Before Tony Stewart hoisted the trophy in Victory Lane for his first victory at Las Vegas (Above), his crew gave him fast pit stops (Opposite page top).

Opposite page bottom: During the contest, Jeff Burton (No. 31) raced to the inside of Trevor Bayne (No. 21) and Jeff Gordon (No. 24) in three-wide action.

■ 04 ■ ■ ■ ■ ■ ■ ■ ■ ■ ■ ■

Bristol Motor Speedway
Sunday, March 18, 2012

FOOD CITY 500

Picking up where he left off in 2011 at Bristol Motor Speedway, Brad Keselowski put a stranglehold on his fellow drivers, leading nearly half the laps on his way to a 'see-ya-later' victory in the Food City 500.

The official margin of victory was 0.714 of a second – a wide margin on the half-mile oval in northeast Tennessee. Keselowski was about eight car lengths ahead of runner-up Matt Kenseth as he flew under the checkered flag.

"Yeah, I mean, what can I say? I love Bristol and Bristol loves me," said Keselowski, who tweeted photographs from Victory Lane. "It's a great track that really demands a hundred percent out of a driver and out of a team."

Martin Truex Jr. finished third, followed by Clint Bowyer and Brian Vickers – all three driving for Michael Waltrip Racing in one of the car owner's strongest efforts yet.

Keselowski led 232 of the 500 laps, including the final 111 circuits. But he had to survive a late-race restart on lap 484 after a yellow flag flew when Tony Stewart smacked the wall in turn three.

Restarting on the outside, Keselowski swept past Daytona 500 winner Matt Kenseth on the backstretch and then held him off through several more corners before stretching out his lead on the way to his fifth career victory.

"I knew as long as I could beat him on the first lap, I knew I had a good enough car and I'm a good enough driver to win," Keselowski said. "Today my team certainly delivered. You could probably argue whether or not I did," he quipped with a smile. "But it was good. My guys, they made it happen today. I told somebody before the race, 'This is the best race car I've ever had in [NASCAR Sprint] Cup.' It showed off today. Hopefully we can have more cars like this and we'll win more races and continue to move the needle forward."

Pole winner Greg Biffle (No. 16) , starting on the outside, leads AJ Allmendinger (No. 22) across the starting line as the green flag falls on the Food City 500 at Bristol Motor Speedway.

Above: NASCAR Sprint Cup Series champion Tony Stewart has a chat with car owner Rick Hendrick, whose racing company supplies the engines for the Chevys of Stewart-Haas Racing.

Opposite page: Marcos Ambrose has both hands on the steering wheel before heading out on the short track at Bristol Motor Speedway.

In August 2011, Keselowski's victory in the night race at Bristol vaulted him into the wild-card spot in the Chase for the NASCAR Sprint Cup.

"We need to keep winning races to lock ourselves in the Chase, but heck, I'd rather just go into the Chase in the top spot," he said. "If we run like we have the last few weeks, we've got as good a shot as anybody else."

The race was largely trouble free except for a seven-car crash on lap 24 that started when Kasey Kahne got into Regan Smith on the frontstretch. Kahne had one of the fastest cars of the weekend, but it all went for naught in his third crash of the young season.

It was a huge race for Vickers, who was making his first start in a part-time arrangement with Waltrip's team. Vickers took full advantage of the opportunity by leading 125 laps – second only to Keselowski – while running with the leaders all day.

"It felt really good when we were out there leading," Vickers said. "It would have been awesome to hold onto that, but it's the first time back so I can't complain about that."

04 | Food City 500

FIN	ST	CAR	DRIVER	SPONSOR	LAPS
1	5	2	Brad Keselowski	Miller Lite Dodge	500
2	21	17	Matt Kenseth	Best Buy Ford	500
3	15	56	Martin Truex Jr	NAPA Auto Parts Toyota	500
4	16	15	Clint Bowyer	5-hour Energy Toyota	500
5	25	55	Brian Vickers	Aaron's Toyota	500
6	33	31	Jeff Burton	BB&T Chevrolet	500
7	17	1	Jamie McMurray	McDonald's Chevrolet	500
8	30	42	Juan Pablo Montoya	Target Chevrolet	500
9	22	48	Jimmie Johnson	Lowe's / Kobalt Tools Chevrolet	500
10	11	27	Paul Menard	Menards / MOEN Chevrolet	500
11	14	29	Kevin Harvick	Budweiser Chevrolet	500
12	3	39	Ryan Newman	Quicken Loans Chevrolet	500
13	1	16	Greg Biffle	811 / 3M Ford	500
14	23	14	Tony Stewart	Office Depot / Mobil 1 Chevrolet	500
15	18	88	Dale Earnhardt Jr	National Guard / Diet Mountain Dew Chevrolet	500
16	9	20	Joey Logano	The Home Depot Toyota	498
17	2	22	AJ Allmendinger	Shell Pennzoil Dodge	498
18	27	51	Kurt Busch	Hendrickcars.com Chevrolet	498
19	7	43	Aric Almirola	Charter Communications Ford	498
20	20	11	Denny Hamlin	FedEx Ground Toyota	498
21	19	10	David Reutimann	TRADEBANK Chevrolet	497
22	32	33	Brendan Gaughan	South Point Hotel & Casino Chevrolet	496
23	31	34	David Ragan	Long John Silver's Ford	496
24	6	78	Regan Smith	Furniture Row Racing / CSX Play It Safe Chevrolet	496
25	24	13	Casey Mears	GEICO Ford	496
26	26	38	David Gilliland	Taco Bell Ford	496
27	34	93	Travis Kvapil	Burger King / Dr. Pepper Toyota	496
28	36	47	Bobby Labonte	Clorox / Scott Products Toyota	495
29	29	83	Landon Cassill	Burger King / Dr. Pepper Toyota	495
30	40	49	J.J. Yeley	JPO Absorbents Toyota	493
31	39	98	Michael McDowell	K LOVE - Let It Start With Me Ford	492
32	13	18	Kyle Busch	Wrigley Doublemint Toyota	423
33	42	32	Ken Schrader	We Drive Sales - TMone.com Ford	420
34	35	36	Dave Blaney	Seal Wrap / Widow Wax Chevrolet	417
35	4	24	Jeff Gordon	Drive to End Hunger Chevrolet	395
36	12	9	Marcos Ambrose	MAC Tools Ford	389
37	10	5	Kasey Kahne	Farmers Insurance Chevrolet	366
38	28	30	David Stremme	Food Country USA / Inception Motorsports Toyota	334
39	8	99	Carl Edwards	Kellogg's / Cheez-It Ford	245
40	41	87	Joe Nemechek	AM/FM Energy Wood & Pellet Stoves Toyota	57
41	43	23	Scott Riggs	North Texas Pipe Chevrolet	26
42	38	74	Reed Sorenson	Carnegie Hotel / Turn One Racing Chevrolet	17
43	37	26	Josh Wise*	Morristown Drivers Service Ford	16

*Sunoco Rookie of the Year Contender

NASCAR Sprint Cup Series

TOP 12
(After 4 Races)

Pos.	Driver	Points	Pos.	Driver	Points
1	GREG BIFFLE	157	7	TONY STEWART	130
2	KEVIN HARVICK	148	8	CLINT BOWYER	126
3	MATT KENSETH	145	9	JOEY LOGANO	126
4	MARTIN TRUEX JR	139	10	PAUL MENARD	123
5	DENNY HAMLIN	137	11	JEFF BURTON	120
6	DALE EARNHARDT JR	137	12	RYAN NEWMAN	118

Above: After winning his second straight race at Bristol, Brad Keselowski (No. 2) burns the back tires off his Dodge during a burnout on the frontstretch.

Opposite page: The action is fast and furious during a round of pit stops under the yellow flag at Bristol.

05

Auto Club Speedway
Sunday, March 25, 2012

AUTO CLUB 400

Tony Stewart is known as a closer. More than two thirds of his NASCAR Sprint Cup Series victories have come in the second half of the year, and all five of his 2011 wins came in the final 10 races during his remarkable run to the championship in the Chase for the NASCAR Sprint Cup.

So when Stewart won the rain-shortened Auto Club 400 at Auto Club Speedway, capturing his second victory of the 2012 season in only five races, he served notice that, if anything, this year his competitors have even more to fear from the defending champion.

Driving his No. 14 Office Depot/Mobil 1 Chevrolet, Stewart led 42 of the final 45 laps in the abbreviated event, which had to be called to a halt after 129 of the scheduled 200 laps. Behind him at the finish was Kyle Busch, who led a race-high 80 laps, followed by Dale Earnhardt Jr., Kevin Harvick and Carl Edwards.

"You hate to have it end with rain like that,"' Stewart said. "But we've lost some that way, and we didn't back into the lead."

And he hasn't skipped a beat following his third NASCAR Sprint Cup championship. His two wins in 2012 have extended 2011's hottest-of-hot-streaks, giving him seven victories in 15 races, despite replacing his championship-winning crew chief, Darian Grubb, with Steve Addington.

"It's been nice to get off to a good start this year the way we have," said Stewart after his 46th career victory. "The history shows that the last 13 years, we haven't had the strongest start the first third of the year, but I'm really excited about the start we've got going. I'm really proud of what Steve and all our guys have done."

The day dawned with southern California's typically blue skies, but a front moving in from the Pacific Ocean gradually

Tony Stewart (No. 14) drives under Jimmie Johnson (No. 48) on his way to his second win in the young 2012 season.

moved further inland. The race ran entirely under the green flag until the rain finally arrived on lap 125.

Pole winner Denny Hamlin led the first lap, but teammate Busch quickly took the lead and was in front for the next 66 laps. Busch was leading on lap 85 when Stewart got past to take the lead.

The greatest beneficiary of the rain, besides Stewart, was Jimmie Johnson, who was running in 10th place when the race had to be stopped, but struggling with a sick engine that was leaking oil. As the rain fell, the red flag came out, and when the cars were brought to pit road, a puddle of oil soon appeared under Johnson's car from a broken oil line. The necessary repairs would have sent Johnson way back in the field, but the rain let him finish 10th.

Greg Biffle, after starting the season with three straight third-place finishes, was sixth in this race, which was good enough to allow him to keep his lead in NASCAR Sprint Cup points for the fourth consecutive race.

05 | Auto Club 400

FIN	ST	CAR	DRIVER	SPONSOR	LAPS
1	9	14	Tony Stewart	Office Depot/Mobil 1 Chevrolet	129
2	2	18	Kyle Busch	Interstate Batteries Toyota	129
3	14	88	Dale Earnhardt Jr	Diet Mountain Dew/National Guard Chevrolet	129
4	7	29	Kevin Harvick	Jimmy John's Chevrolet	129
5	12	99	Carl Edwards	Subway Ford	129
6	4	16	Greg Biffle	3M Ford	129
7	6	39	Ryan Newman	U.S. ARMY Chevrolet	129
8	13	56	Martin Truex Jr	NAPA Auto Parts Toyota	129
9	23	51	Kurt Busch	Phoenix Construction Services Inc. Chevrolet	129
10	10	48	Jimmie Johnson	Lowe's/Jimmie Johnson Foundation Chevrolet	129
11	1	11	Denny Hamlin	FedEx Express Toyota	129
12	3	55	Mark Martin	Aaron's Toyota	129
13	11	15	Clint Bowyer	5-hour Energy Toyota	129
14	5	5	Kasey Kahne	Quaker State Chevrolet	129
15	25	22	AJ Allmendinger	Southern California AAA Dodge	129
16	15	17	Matt Kenseth	Ford EcoBoost Ford	129
17	24	42	Juan Pablo Montoya	Target Chevrolet	128
18	17	2	Brad Keselowski	Miller Lite Dodge	128
19	27	27	Paul Menard	Menards/CertainTeed Chevrolet	128
20	22	78	Regan Smith	Furniture Row/Farm American Chevrolet	128
21	29	9	Marcos Ambrose	DeWalt Ford	128
22	19	31	Jeff Burton	Caterpillar Chevrolet	128
23	33	13	Casey Mears	GEICO Ford	128
24	8	20	Joey Logano	Dollar General Toyota	128
25	28	43	Aric Almirola	Medallion Financial Ford	128
26	21	24	Jeff Gordon	Drive to End Hunger Chevrolet	128
27	18	10	David Reutimann	Accell Construction Chevrolet	127
28	26	47	Bobby Labonte	Charter Toyota	127
29	40	93	Travis Kvapil	Burger King/Dr. Pepper Toyota	127
30	41	38	David Gilliland	1-800 LoanMart Ford	127
31	38	34	David Ragan	Front Row Motorsports Ford	127
32	16	1	Jamie McMurray	Bass Pro Shops/Allstate Chevrolet	126
33	34	36	Dave Blaney	Tommy Baldwin Racing Chevrolet	126
34	42	32	Ken Schrader	US Chrome/1 Less Than 2 Ltd. Ford	125
35	36	49	J.J. Yeley	America Israel Racing Chevrolet	125
36	31	83	Landon Cassill	Burger King/Dr. Pepper Toyota	124
37	30	26	Josh Wise*	MDS Ford	51
38	32	98	Michael McDowell	Curb Records Ford	40
39	20	30	David Stremme	@TheNascarFans Toyota	36
40	39	19	Mike Bliss	Ironclad Toyota	18
41	35	23	Scott Riggs	North TX Pipe Chevrolet	17
42	43	74	Reed Sorenson	Turn One Racing Chevrolet	6
43	37	33	Brendan Gaughan	South Point Casino Chevrolet	1

*Sunoco Rookie of the Year Contender

NASCAR Sprint Cup Series — TOP 12
(After 5 Races)

Pos.	Driver	Points	Pos.	Driver	Points
1	GREG BIFFLE	195	7	DENNY HAMLIN	171
2	KEVIN HARVICK	188	8	CLINT BOWYER	157
3	DALE EARNHARDT JR	178	9	JIMMIE JOHNSON	156
4	TONY STEWART	177	10	RYAN NEWMAN	155
5	MARTIN TRUEX JR	175	11	PAUL MENARD	148
6	MATT KENSETH	173	12	CARL EDWARDS	146

Above: Stewart's (No. 14) race-winning crew are two tires deep into a four-tire pit stop at Auto Club Speedway.

Opposite page: (Top) Kevin Harvick and Ryan Newman share a rooftop during a break in the action in southern California. (Bottom) Jeff Gordon's No. 24 Drive to End Hunger Chevy sits in the Auto Club Speedway garage with its hood up, ready for service.

06

GOODY'S FAST RELIEF 500

The finish of the Goody's Fast Relief 500 was already fixing to be a barn-burner between Hendrick Motorsports teammates Jimmie Johnson and Jeff Gordon, but as they battled side-by-side for the lead with four laps to go, harsh fate intervened, turned the race upside down and handed the victory to Ryan Newman.

Gordon had dominated the race, leading 329 laps, before giving way to Johnson, who led 111 of the final 150 laps. But as the laps wound down, Gordon edged ever closer to Johnson's back bumper. With six laps to go, he went inside for the first time. And with four laps to go, they battled side by side down the frontstretch, with Gordon edging ahead to retake the lead. At that moment, the yellow flag came out.

In the ensuing green-white-checkered overtime finish, Clint Bowyer tried to barge into the lead and ended up taking himself out along with Johnson and Gordon. Newman, who had restarted fifth, hugged the curb in Martinsville's tight second turn, shot past the melee at full speed and took the lead as the yellow flag came back out.

Newman then held off AJ Allmendinger in the second green-white-checkered finish to win his 16th career victory. Dale Earnhardt Jr. finished third, followed by Matt Kenseth and Martin Truex Jr.

"We were not a dominant race car today but we put ourselves in contention," Newman said in the winner's interview. "The way the strategy and everything worked out, coming in for two tires (during the final pit stop) and Clint kind of clearing out turn one for us, we were fortunate to be in the right place at the right time."

Gordon and Johnson had led a combined 440 laps, with Gordon in front more than twice as much. And it appeared that Gordon was finally going to regain the upper hand until

With Aric Almirola (No. 43) and Dale Earnhardt Jr. (No. 88) leading the way, the drivers battle side-by-side around the tight Martinsville oval.

David Reutimann's car stopped as he tried to limp to the finish, earning him and his team the ire of fellow competitors and NASCAR.

"The thing quit going down the back straightaway, and it shut off," Reutimann said. "I just didn't stop there intentionally. I hate it for everybody that it affected, but I mean I can't get out and push the thing."

During the caution period that Reutimann caused, both Gordon and Johnson stayed out on the track, while lead-lap drivers behind them pitted and took on fresh tires. As the green flag fell for the first overtime, Gordon and Johnson headed to the first turn side-by-side. Behind them, Bowyer and Brad Keselowski got much better restarts on their new tires, and Bowyer dove to the inside of Gordon, who was still two-wide with Johnson. So they went three-wide into turn one at Martinsville, which is a formula for disaster. As all three cars spun, Keselowski had to slow, but Newman had a clear path on the bottom, and took the lead for the first time in the race as the yellow came back out.

For the second overtime finish, "it was just a matter of racing AJ clean on that next restart," Newman said. "I felt like I wasn't racing AJ on that restart. I felt like I was racing Junior behind me because I didn't want the same thing to happen, because I've seen it happen so many times here. It was really important for me to not spin my tires and get a good start and race AJ and try to eliminate the 88 from the race for the win."

06 | Goody's Fast Relief 500

FIN	ST	CAR	DRIVER	SPONSOR	LAPS
1	5	39	Ryan Newman	Outback Steakhouse Chevrolet	515
2	27	22	AJ Allmendinger	Shell Pennzoil Dodge	515
3	14	88	Dale Earnhardt Jr	AMP Energy/Diet Mtn. Dew/Nat'l Guard Chevrolet	515
4	21	17	Matt Kenseth	Stephen Siller Tunnel to Towers/Sinise Foun. Ford	515
5	13	56	Martin Truex Jr	NAPA Auto Parts Toyota	515
6	3	11	Denny Hamlin	FedEx Freight Toyota	515
7	15	14	Tony Stewart	Office Depot/Mobil 1 Chevrolet	515
8	19	43	Aric Almirola	Smithfield Helping Hungry Homes Ford	515
9	7	2	Brad Keselowski	Miller Lite Dodge	515
10	4	15	Clint Bowyer	5-hour Energy Toyota	515
11	28	99	Carl Edwards	Fastenal Ford	515
12	22	48	Jimmie Johnson	myLowes Chevrolet	515
13	26	16	Greg Biffle	3M Ford	514
14	9	24	Jeff Gordon	Drive to End Hunger Chevrolet	514
15	12	9	Marcos Ambrose	DeWalt Ford	513
16	17	78	Regan Smith	Furniture Row Racing/CSX Play It Safe Chevrolet	513
17	16	47	Bobby Labonte	Bush's Best Beans Toyota	513
18	6	55	Brian Vickers	RKMotorsCharlotte.com/Aaron's Toyota	513
19	2	29	Kevin Harvick	Budweiser is Back Chevrolet	513
20	20	1	Jamie McMurray	Belkin Chevrolet	513
21	32	42	Juan Pablo Montoya	Target Chevrolet	512
22	18	31	Jeff Burton	BB&T Chevrolet	512
23	10	20	Joey Logano	The Home Depot Toyota	511
24	24	34	David Ragan	Front Row Motorsports Ford	511
25	25	13	Casey Mears	GEICO Ford	511
26	11	27	Paul Menard	Menards/LIBMAN Chevrolet	510
27	34	93	Travis Kvapil	Burger King/Dr. Pepper Toyota	510
28	38	38	David Gilliland	Long John Silver's Ford	509
29	31	83	Landon Cassill	Burger King/Dr. Pepper Toyota	507
30	39	30	David Stremme	Inception Motorsports Toyota	506
31	41	33	Hermie Sadler	Anderson's Pure Maple Syrup Chevrolet	505
32	36	32	Ken Schrader	Federated Auto Parts Ford	503
33	40	51	Kurt Busch	Phoenix Construction Services Chevrolet	497
34	42	36	Dave Blaney	Ollie's Bargain Outlet Chevrolet	439
35	29	10	David Reutimann	Accell Construction Chevrolet	436
36	8	18	Kyle Busch	M&M's Toyota	435
37	43	49	J.J. Yeley	America Israel Racing/JPO Absorbents Toyota	359
38	1	5	Kasey Kahne	Hendrickcars.com Chevrolet	256
39	37	87	Joe Nemechek	AM/FM Energy Wood & Pellet Stoves Toyota	74
40	23	98	Michael McDowell	Curb Records Ford	60
41	30	26	Josh Wise*	Morristown Drivers Service Ford	49
42	33	23	Scott Riggs	North Texas Pipe Chevrolet	30
43	35	74	Reed Sorenson	Turn One Racing Chevrolet	25

*Sunoco Rookie of the Year Contender

NASCAR Sprint Cup Series **TOP 12** (After 6 Races)

Pos.	Driver	Points	Pos.	Driver	Points
1	GREG BIFFLE	226	7	DENNY HAMLIN	210
2	DALE EARNHARDT JR	220	8	RYAN NEWMAN	202
3	TONY STEWART	214	9	CLINT BOWYER	192
4	MATT KENSETH	214	10	JIMMIE JOHNSON	189
5	KEVIN HARVICK	214	11	CARL EDWARDS	179
6	MARTIN TRUEX JR	214	12	BRAD KESELOWSKI	175

Above: With his Victory Lane celebration reflected through the scoreboard monitor, Ryan Newman celebrates his first victory at Martinsville Speedway.

Opposite page: Two of Martinsville's most faithful fans advertise their favorite drivers in face paint.

07

Texas Motor Speedway
Saturday, April 14, 2012

SAMSUNG MOBILE 500

Already atop the NASCAR Sprint Cup Series points standings by virtue of his fast start in the 2012 season, Greg Biffle felt like it was only a matter of time before he picked the lock on the gate to Victory Lane.

"We've been running so good," Biffle said. "We've had great pit stops. We've had good cars."

And it was, finally, time for the Biff in the Samsung Mobile 500 at Texas Motor Speedway, as he cruised to victory by 3.235 seconds over Jimmie Johnson after leading the final 31 laps. Ageless veteran Mark Martin finished third, followed by Jeff Gordon and Matt Kenseth. With the victory, his second at Texas, Biffle broke a 49-race winless streak and posted his 17th career win. It was the Roush Fenway Racing veteran's first victory since winning at Kansas late in the 2010 season.

"I'll tell you what, I could say it's about time, but hard work pays off still today, and that's what this is about, the team and (crew chief) Matt Puccia putting together the guys he has, the engine shop, how hard they've worked on the fuel injection and the engines and all that," Biffle said. "I am just thankful to get the opportunity to drive these cars as fast as they are. We knew it was a matter of time we were going to win one of these things."

Although Biffle led more than 30 laps early in the race in his No. 16 Filtrete Ford, Johnson took over and eventually led 156 laps, the most of anyone. But in the final stages, Biffle came back for the kill. With 31 laps to go, he dove down hard into turn three and steered under Johnson and into the lead. He pulled away from there.

"I just dug deep. I knew I had to do it and kept trying and trying and trying," Biffle said. "I knew the team would forgive me if I wrecked it trying to beat him so I just gave it all I had.

The pit crew for Martin Truex Jr. (No. 56) services his NAPA Auto Parts Toyota during the Samsung Mobile 500. Truex led 69 laps before slipping to a sixth-place finish.

Catching the 48 at the end, it was all I had to be able to get to him," he said. "It seemed like when we got to him, it was too easy. I was surprised I didn't have to deal with him anymore, though. I thought he was going to be right there, and he was for a little bit, but once I got out front like that, then I was able to pull away from him."

Johnson tried to keep up, but any chance of that ended when he nicked the wall trying to get more speed out of his Chevy.

"I'm definitely disappointed, but we had a great race car and there's a lot to be proud of here today," Johnson said. "We had a very, very fast race car and a little bit more respect through some lapped traffic could've been a little different. I just got tangled up in some lapped traffic and the 16 made a great move and got by me. And then I was chasing him from there and didn't have anything left to go get him. I tried and ran out of grip going into turn three and drilled the fence, but I brought it home in second. Certainly wish we were over there in Victory Lane but everybody knows we're here," Johnson added. "We're awfully close to it with this Kobalt Tools Chevrolet."

So the tables were turned, and the five-time NASCAR Sprint Cup champion was the one on the outside looking in.

"Yeah, it'll wear on you," said Biffle, who's had plenty of experience doing that. "You know, it'll take years off your life. I've probably lost several. But you know what, I've been doing this deal a long time, and what kept me going or what keeps your spirit up is when you ran good."

07 | Samsung Mobile 500

FIN	ST	CAR	DRIVER	SPONSOR	LAPS
1	3	16	Greg Biffle	Filtrete Ford	334
2	10	48	Jimmie Johnson	Lowe's/Kobalt Tools Chevrolet	334
3	4	55	Mark Martin	Aaron's Best of the Best Toyota	334
4	34	24	Jeff Gordon	DuPont Chevrolet	334
5	2	17	Matt Kenseth	Best Buy Ford	334
6	1	56	Martin Truex Jr	NAPA Auto Parts Toyota	334
7	5	5	Kasey Kahne	Farmers Insurance Chevrolet	334
8	20	99	Carl Edwards	Fastenal Ford	334
9	15	29	Kevin Harvick	Budweiser Chevrolet	334
10	16	88	Dale Earnhardt Jr	Diet Mountain Dew/National Guard Chevrolet	334
11	17	18	Kyle Busch	Interstate Batteries Toyota	334
12	13	11	Denny Hamlin	FedEx Office/March of Dimes Toyota	334
13	27	51	Kurt Busch	Phoenix Construction Services, Inc. Chevrolet	333
14	9	1	Jamie McMurray	Bass Pro Shops/Tracker Boats Chevrolet	333
15	12	22	AJ Allmendinger	Shell Pennzoil Dodge	333
16	25	42	Juan Pablo Montoya	Target Chevrolet	333
17	18	15	Clint Bowyer	5-hour Energy Toyota	333
18	11	27	Paul Menard	Quaker State/Menards Chevrolet	333
19	14	20	Joey Logano	Dollar General Toyota	333
20	7	9	Marcos Ambrose	Stanley Ford	333
21	6	39	Ryan Newman	US ARMY Chevrolet	332
22	23	43	Aric Almirola	Smithfield Ford	332
23	26	78	Regan Smith	Furniture Row/Farm American Chevrolet	332
24	29	14	Tony Stewart	Mobil 1 Adv'd Fuel Economy/Office Depot Chev	332
25	22	13	Casey Mears	GEICO Ford	331
26	31	10	David Reutimann	Accell Construction Chevrolet	331
27	30	47	Bobby Labonte	Bush's Beans/Tom Thumb Toyota	330
28	19	21	Trevor Bayne	Motorcraft/Quick Lane Tire & Auto Center Ford	330
29	24	31	Jeff Burton	Caterpillar Chevrolet	330
30	28	83	Landon Cassill	Burger King/Dr. Pepper Toyota	330
31	35	38	David Gilliland	Mod Space Ford	328
32	39	32	Reed Sorenson	JaniKing Ford	327
33	36	49	J.J. Yeley	JPO Absorbents Toyota	325
34	42	33	Tony Raines	Precon Marine Chevrolet	323
35	21	34	David Ragan	Scorpion Truck Bed Liners Ford	313
36	8	2	Brad Keselowski	Miller Lite Dodge	312
37	41	36	Dave Blaney	Jimmie Johnson's Anything With An Engine Chev	228
38	37	93	Travis Kvapil	Dr. Pepper Toyota	114
39	32	26	Josh Wise*	Morristown Driver's Service Ford	66
40	43	19	Mike Bliss	Humphrey Smith Racing, LLC Toyota	38
41	33	98	Michael McDowell	Curb Records Ford	36
42	40	23	Scott Riggs	North TX Pipe/Embassy Suites Chevrolet	25
43	38	95	Scott Speed	TWD Drywall Ford	13

*Sunoco Rookie of the Year Contender

NASCAR Sprint Cup Series **TOP 12** (After 7 Races)

Pos.	Driver	Points	Pos.	Driver	Points
1	GREG BIFFLE	273	7	TONY STEWART	234
2	MATT KENSETH	254	8	JIMMIE JOHNSON	233
3	DALE EARNHARDT JR	254	9	RYAN NEWMAN	225
4	MARTIN TRUEX JR	253	10	CLINT BOWYER	219
5	KEVIN HARVICK	249	11	CARL EDWARDS	215
6	DENNY HAMLIN	242	12	PAUL MENARD	192

Previous spread: Pole sitter Martin Truex Jr. (No. 56), with Matt Kenseth (No. 17) on the outside, leads the 43-car field to the green flag to start the Samsung Mobile 500.

Opposite page: Matt Kenseth, who led 15 laps before finishing fifth, reaches across Greg Biffle's No. 16 Filtrete Ford to congratulate the race winner in Victory Lane.

Above: In the garage at Texas Motor Speedway, Kyle Busch checks some information on a mobile device.

08

Kansas Speedway
Sunday, April 22, 2012

STP 400

When the sun finally forced its way through the clouds that covered the Kansas sky most of the day, Denny Hamlin found some speed just as dominant Martin Truex Jr. lost some, winning the STP 400 at Kansas Speedway by 0.70 of a second to capture his second race of the still-young season.

Pouring it on in his No. 11 FedEx Ground Toyota, Hamlin dove to the low groove in turns three and four as Truex stayed in the high groove with 31 laps to go. As they emerged together out of turn four, Hamlin was in front. And he stretched it out from there, although with three laps to go and again on the final lap, Truex made valiant but futile attempts to pass, nearly losing control of his car in the process.

Jimmie Johnson finished third, followed by Matt Kenseth and Greg Biffle in a largely trouble-free race that saw only three yellow flags – two for debris on the track and one for a single-car spin.

"Whether it was a coincidence or not, the car, to the field, was better once the sun came out," Hamlin said after his 19th career victory, but his first at Kansas. "I felt like our car lost a lot of grip when the sun came out, but I guess a lot of guys did when that happened."

Losing grip, Hamlin said, was an advantage to him. "Typically, when you have an overcast condition, the cars run a little bit tighter (and) the grip level is higher in the race car," he said. "So it's more of a track position type race when there's overcast conditions. When the sun is out, the drivers, in my opinion, are more prominent. Your driver can move around, find the grip, do things in the car to make up for what his car doesn't have. So the slicker the conditions are, the better it tends to lead to our race team, and luckily we had that run in

Race winner Denny Hamlin (No. 11) cooks his tires doing a burnout on the frontstretch at Kansas Speedway after finishing first in the STP 400.

the sunshine."

Truex, who led 173 of the 267 laps in his No. 56 NAPA Auto Parts Toyota, often by large margins over the rest of the field, said his car lost its edge after the last pit stop. "We had 'em," Truex said.

"I don't know what happened with that last set of tires, they were terrible. I couldn't go at all – was just dead sideways, wrecking. At the end of the run, I was back to being okay again, but by then, he (Hamlin) had already passed me and clean air is everything."

"I don't think it was the sun," Truex said. "We put that last set of tires on and it wasn't anything like it had been all day long – just bad, bad loose for the first 20 laps of that run."

Biffle's fifth-place finish, his fifth top-five in the season's first eight races, kept him in front in the NASCAR Sprint Cup Series points lead, 15 points ahead of Truex.

08 | STP 400

FIN	ST	CAR	DRIVER	SPONSOR	LAPS
1	4	11	Denny Hamlin	FedEx Ground Toyota	267
2	6	56	Martin Truex Jr	NAPA Auto Parts Toyota	267
3	15	48	Jimmie Johnson	Lowe's Chevrolet	267
4	18	17	Matt Kenseth	Ford EcoBoost Ford	267
5	17	16	Greg Biffle	3M Novec 1230 Ford	267
6	2	29	Kevin Harvick	Rheem Chevrolet	267
7	7	88	Dale Earnhardt Jr	Diet Mountain Dew/National Guard Chevrolet	267
8	9	5	Kasey Kahne	Farmers Insurance Chevrolet	267
9	21	99	Carl Edwards	Aflac Ford	267
10	25	18	Kyle Busch	M&M's Toyota	267
11	11	2	Brad Keselowski	Miller Lite Dodge	267
12	39	42	Juan Pablo Montoya	Target Chevrolet	267
13	23	14	Tony Stewart	Office Depot/Mobil 1 Chevrolet	267
14	36	1	Jamie McMurray	McDonald's Chevrolet	266
15	3	20	Joey Logano	The Home Depot Toyota	266
16	28	9	Marcos Ambrose	DeWalt Ford	266
17	14	51	Kurt Busch	Phoenix Construction Services, Inc. Chevrolet	266
18	19	27	Paul Menard	Menards/Zecol Chevrolet	266
19	10	12	Sam Hornish Jr	SKF Dodge	266
20	13	39	Ryan Newman	Haas Automation Chevrolet	265
21	20	24	Jeff Gordon	Drive to End Hunger Chevrolet	264
22	12	31	Jeff Burton	Caterpillar Chevrolet	264
23	26	43	Aric Almirola	STP Ford	264
24	29	78	Regan Smith	Furniture Row/Farm American Chevrolet	263
25	35	93	Travis Kvapil	Burger King Real Fruit Smoothies Toyota	263
26	40	13	Casey Mears	GEICO Ford	263
27	22	38	David Gilliland	Front Row Motorsports Ford	263
28	42	32	Reed Sorenson	@TMone We Drive Sales/FAS Lane Ford	263
29	16	10	David Reutimann	Accell Construction Chevrolet	262
30	27	34	David Ragan	Barrett-Jackson Ford	262
31	31	49	J.J. Yeley	JPO Absorbents Toyota	261
32	1	22	AJ Allmendinger	AAA Dodge	257
33	5	55	Mark Martin	Aaron's Dream Machine Toyota	255
34	32	83	Landon Cassill	Burger King Real Fruit Smoothies Toyota	214
35	30	47	Bobby Labonte	Reese Towpower Toyota	132
36	8	15	Clint Bowyer	5-hour Energy Toyota	125
37	33	36	Dave Blaney	Tommy Baldwin Racing Chevrolet	82
38	24	30	David Stremme	Inception Motorsports Toyota	80
39	38	26	Josh Wise*	Morristown Driver's Service Ford	65
40	37	98	Michael McDowell	Curb Records Ford	58
41	41	87	Joe Nemechek	AM/FM Energy Wood & Pellet Stoves Toyota	47
42	43	19	Mike Bliss	Humphrey Smith Racing LLC Toyota	27
43	34	23	Scott Riggs	North TX Pipe Chevrolet	18

*Sunoco Rookie of the Year Contender

NASCAR Sprint Cup Series TOP 12

(After 8 Races)

Pos.	Driver	Points	Pos.	Driver	Points
1	GREG BIFFLE	312	7	JIMMIE JOHNSON	275
2	MARTIN TRUEX JR	297	8	TONY STEWART	265
3	MATT KENSETH	295	9	CARL EDWARDS	251
4	DALE EARNHARDT JR	291	10	RYAN NEWMAN	249
5	DENNY HAMLIN	289	11	CLINT BOWYER	227
6	KEVIN HARVICK	287	12	JOEY LOGANO	221

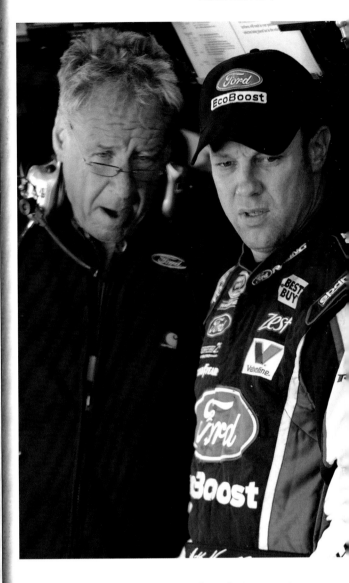

Previous spread: The action is fast, furious and three-wide at the 1.5-mile Kansas Speedway.

Opposite page left: Dale Earnhardt Jr. stays warm on a chilly pit road wearing a sweatshirt.

Opposite page right: During the race, pit crews were busy up and down pit road at Kansas.

Above: Matt Kenseth, who finished fourth in the race, consults Jimmy Fennig, his veteran Roush Fenway Racing crew chief, in the garage during a practice session.

09

Richmond International Raceway
Saturday, April 28, 2012

CAPITAL CITY 400
PRESENTED BY VIRGINIA IS FOR LOVERS

Kyle Busch has a knack for dominating weekends and dominating race tracks, and both talents were on display at Richmond International Raceway when he notched his first victory as a car owner in the NASCAR Nationwide Series and then went out and won his fourth consecutive Capital City 400 Presented by Virginia is for Lovers.

The evening before Busch's NASCAR Sprint Cup Series victory, older brother Kurt drove the Kyle Busch Motorsports Toyota to its first series victory, leading the final 29 laps before beating Kyle's Joe Gibbs Racing's teammate, Denny Hamlin, by a few cars lengths.

Kyle Busch had dominated at Richmond a year earlier, leading more than half the laps in an easy victory. This one was not so cut and dried. He only led 32 laps, and he could not have won were it not for a late-race yellow flag that gave him a fighting chance, and a fast final pit stop that put him in the lead.

"It was a gift," Busch said of the final caution, which flew for debris on lap 388. "Man, I just don't know where it came from or what it was or anything, but it doesn't matter. We came down pit road and (crew chief) Dave Rogers and these guys went to work and gave me a great pit stop (and) got me out front."

Busch led the final 13 laps before winning by 1.095 seconds over Dale Earnhardt Jr. Tony Stewart was third, followed by Denny Hamlin and Kasey Kahne. It was Busch's first win of the 2012 season and his 24th career victory. Points leader Greg Biffle finished 18th, but retained a five-point lead over Earnhardt Jr.

Busch started fifth but didn't lead in his No. 18 M&M's Brown Toyota until lap 286 of the 400-lap contest around Richmond's ¾-mile oval. It was Carl Edwards who was show-

---

Race fans high in the grandstands along the frontstretch of Richmond International Raceway enjoyed a panoramic view of the entire ¾-mile track during the Capital City 400 Presented by Virginia is for Lovers.

ing his back bumper to the rest of the field, leading 202 of the first 250 laps.

But Edwards's chance for victory faded with 81 laps to go when he was penalized for jumping a restart while positioned next to Stewart, who was leading.

Stewart dominated much of the rest of the race, but his comfortable lead was erased by that final yellow flag.

"When the caution is for a plastic bottle on the backstretch, it's hard to feel good losing that one," Stewart said. "And we gave it away on pit road. So we did everything we could to throw it away."

Busch was strongest on the short runs and Stewart was bet-

ter on the long runs, so Busch easily pulled away from him after the restart with nine laps to go. Earnhardt also got around Stewart before the finish.

But before the yellow, Stewart was untouchable.

"No catching Stewart without that caution," Busch said. "I was losing half a tenth to a tenth on every lap to what Tony was doing up there. He was just so fast. Stewart was phenomenal. I hate it for him that we had a caution like that. He deserved to win the race. But I can't say enough about us just getting our lucky break there and getting a chance to win. They gave me a great pit stop, got me out front (and) gave me the lead so I could restart the race how I wanted to. That was the win right there."

09 | CAPITAL CITY 400
PRESENTED BY VIRGINIA IS FOR LOVERS

FIN	ST	CAR	DRIVER	SPONSOR	LAPS
1	5	18	Kyle Busch	M&M's Brown Toyota	400
2	10	88	Dale Earnhardt Jr	National Guard / Diet Mountain Dew Chevrolet	400
3	22	14	Tony Stewart	MOBIL 1 / Office Depot Chevrolet	400
4	7	11	Denny Hamlin	FedEx Freight Toyota	400
5	9	5	Kasey Kahne	Farmers Insurance Chevrolet	400
6	27	48	Jimmie Johnson	Lowe's Chevrolet	400
7	23	15	Clint Bowyer	5-hour Energy Toyota	400
8	1	55	Mark Martin	Aaron's Dream Machine Toyota	400
9	16	2	Brad Keselowski	Miller Lite Dodge	400
10	2	99	Carl Edwards	Ford EcoBoost Ford	400
11	24	17	Matt Kenseth	Ford EcoBoost Ford	400
12	20	42	Juan Pablo Montoya	Target Chevrolet	400
13	31	27	Paul Menard	Menards / NIBCO Chevrolet	400
14	37	1	Jamie McMurray	McDonald's Chevrolet	400
15	12	39	Ryan Newman	Army Reserve Chevrolet	400
16	4	22	AJ Allmendinger	Shell Pennzoil Dodge	400
17	19	47	Bobby Labonte	Bush's Beans Toyota	400
18	28	16	Greg Biffle	3M / GKAS Ford	400
19	3	29	Kevin Harvick	Jimmy John's Chevrolet	400
20	21	83	Landon Cassill	Burger King / Dr. Pepper Toyota	399
21	26	13	Casey Mears	GEICO Ford	399
22	14	9	Marcos Ambrose	Stanley Ford	399
23	6	24	Jeff Gordon	DuPont Chevrolet	399
24	18	20	Joey Logano	The Home Depot Toyota	399
25	8	56	Martin Truex Jr	NAPA Brakes Toyota	399
26	11	43	Aric Almirola	Smithfield Helping Hungry Homes Ford	398
27	15	78	Regan Smith	Furniture Row Racing / Farm American Chevrolet	398
28	13	51	Kurt Busch	Phoenix Construction Services Chevrolet	397
29	17	36	Dave Blaney	SealWrap.com Chevrolet	397
30	29	93	Travis Kvapil	Burger King / Dr. Pepper Toyota	397
31	30	31	Jeff Burton	BB&T Chevrolet	396
32	38	34	David Ragan	Front Row Motorsports Ford	394
33	33	10	David Reutimann	Tommy Baldwin Racing Chevrolet	394
34	42	32	Reed Sorenson	Virginia Faith & Freedom Coalition Ford	392
35	40	33	Stephen Leicht	LittleJoesAutos.com / Link-Belt Chevrolet	391
36	41	38	David Gilliland	Long John Silver's Ford	355
37	34	30	David Stremme	Inception Motorsports Toyota	139
38	32	26	Josh Wise*	Morristown Drivers Service Ford	127
39	25	98	Michael McDowell	Curb Records Ford	67
40	43	74	Cole Whitt	Turn One Racing Chevrolet	29
41	35	87	Joe Nemechek	AM/FM Energy Wood & Pellet Stoves Toyota	28
42	39	19	Mike Bliss	Humphrey Smith Racing Toyota	23
43	36	95	Scott Speed	TWD Drywall Ford	19

*Sunoco Rookie of the Year Contender

NASCAR Sprint Cup Series **TOP 12** (After 9 Races)

Pos.	Driver	Points	Pos.	Driver	Points
1	GREG BIFFLE	338	7	KEVIN HARVICK	313
2	DALE EARNHARDT JR	333	8	TONY STEWART	307
3	DENNY HAMLIN	329	9	CARL EDWARDS	287
4	MATT KENSETH	328	10	RYAN NEWMAN	278
5	MARTIN TRUEX JR	316	11	KYLE BUSCH	265
6	JIMMIE JOHNSON	314	12	CLINT BOWYER	264

Opposite page: Pole winner Mark Martin (No. 55) leads the field into the first turn to start the race as Kevin Harvick (No. 29) dives to the inside and Carl Edwards (No. 99) works the outside.

Above: With the tire smoke from his victory burnout lingering in the distance, Kyle Busch stands on his car as he celebrates his first win of the 2012 season.

10

Talladega Superspeedway
Sunday, May 6, 2012

AARON'S 499

In the nights before the Aaron's 499, alone in his motor home in the infield at Talladega Superspeedway, 28-year-old bachelor Brad Keselowski thought long and hard about what to do if he was the unfortunate 'sitting duck' leading the race going into the last lap.

In most races, a driver wants to be leading as the white flag flies. At Talladega, in recent years, it often means you're the loser in a spectacular side-by-side finish. It's a long way down that frontstretch to the finish line, which means the second-place driver has more time and space to make a slingshot pass to glory.

As it happened, Keselowski was in exactly that predicament as the white flag flew in a thrill-a-minute Aaron's 499 at Talladega for a green-white-checkered overtime finish. He was leading the race in his No. 2 Miller Lite Dodge, and on his bumper was the hungry and aggressive Kyle Busch, ready to pounce when the cars came out of turn four.

Having thought about what move he might possibly make to foil the attack, and having rehearsed it in his mind, Keselowski was ready. And as he hit turn three with Busch on his bumper, Keselowski tweaked his steering wheel to the right and took his car to the top of the track in hopes of breaking the lock that Busch had on his bumper in the draft. The only hitch to that strategy is that you leave the lower part of the turn completely open to a potential pass.

But as tens of thousands of cheering fans in the grandstands could well see, the move worked to perfection. Busch lost that tight draft he had on Keselowski for just a few moments, but it was enough to thwart any hopes of a successful slingshot pass down the frontstretch. Keselowski beat Busch by 0.304 of a second while Matt Kenseth, Kasey Kahne and Greg Biffle followed to round out the top five. It was Ke-

It's a three-wide battle on the high banks of Talladega Superspeedway as Kyle Busch (No. 18) runs below Casey Mears (No. 13) and Jamie McMurray (No. 1), with Kevin Harvick (No. 29) trailing McMurray and Michael Waltrip (No. 55) below him.

selowski's second victory of the season and the sixth of his NASCAR Sprint Cup Series career, now in its third full year. Biffle's finish kept him atop the NASCAR Sprint Cup championship standings, seven points head of Kenseth.

The trick that Keselowski came up with is exactly the sort of secret strategy that the late Dale Earnhardt would never talk about, but the frank and personable young Penske Racing driver was more than happy to examine the subject in detail.

"You got to have a plan, have the moves ready," Keselowski said. "I just needed to make the move. Made it in (turn) three. That disconnected us. That was the key right there. That allowed me to drive untouched to the checkered flag. It wasn't easy to convince myself to do that, but it was the right move. Once we got that air bubble in between the two cars, it was going to take two or three laps for him to pop that. Only had to go half a lap, not even quite that."

"I had this whole plan if I ever got in that situation where I was leading; I thought about it and thought about it, dreamed about what to do, and sure enough, going into (turn) three, it was just me and Kyle."

To get to that point, Keselowski had to survive a race that featured 33 lead changes among 17 drivers. The race was accident free until a nine-car crash in turn three on lap 143. There were two smaller incidents before another semi-big one – also a nine-car crash – in turn one. That last incident happened on lap 185 of the scheduled 188 laps, taking the race into the overtime finish and setting the stage for Keselowski's well-thought-out move.

"Those are the kind of moves. . . that you get one chance to make," Keselowski said in the winner's interview. "I'm sure everybody will wise up on it from here and they'll make their moves earlier, which will change the racing again. It's just evolution. You get one shot to be that guy that helps to evolve it. We had the opportunity to do that today and that's part of what helped us win the race."

FIN	ST	CAR	DRIVER	SPONSOR	LAPS
1	13	2	Brad Keselowski	Miller Lite Dodge	194
2	21	18	Kyle Busch	M&M's Toyota	194
3	10	17	Matt Kenseth	Best Buy Ford	194
4	5	5	Kasey Kahne	Farmers Insurance Chevrolet	194
5	6	16	Greg Biffle	3M/O'Reilly Auto Parts Ford	194
6	24	15	Clint Bowyer	Aaron's/Alabama National Championship Toyota	194
7	32	34	David Ragan	Front Row Motorsports Ford	194
8	11	21	Trevor Bayne	Motorcraft/Quick Lane Tire & Auto Center Ford	194
9	18	88	Dale Earnhardt Jr	National Guard/Diet Mountain Dew Chevrolet	194
10	29	31	Jeff Burton	Caterpillar Chevrolet	194
11	23	1	Jamie McMurray	Bass Pro Shops/Tracker Boats Chevrolet	194
12	4	43	Aric Almirola	VeriFone Sail Ford	194
13	26	38	David Gilliland	Taco Bell Ford	194
14	3	9	Marcos Ambrose	Stanley Ford	194
15	2	22	AJ Allmendinger	Shell Pennzoil/AAA Dodge	194
16	41	93	Travis Kvapil	Burger King/Dr. Pepper Toyota	194
17	17	27	Paul Menard	Menards/Turtle Wax Chevrolet	194
18	25	13	Casey Mears	GEICO Ford	194
19	9	55	Michael Waltrip	Aaron's Color Your Way Toyota	194
20	33	51	Kurt Busch	Phoenix Construction Services Inc. Chevrolet	193
21	42	47	Bobby Labonte	Bush's Beans Toyota	192
22	34	10	David Reutimann	Tommy Baldwin Racing Chevrolet	192
23	22	11	Denny Hamlin	FedEx Express Toyota	192
24	8	14	Tony Stewart	Office Depot/Mobil 1 Chevrolet	190
25	20	29	Kevin Harvick	Rheem Chevrolet	184
26	30	20	Joey Logano	Dollar General Toyota	184
27	39	23	Robert Richardson	North TX Pipe Toyota	182
28	15	56	Martin Truex Jr	NAPA Auto Parts Toyota	166
29	28	32	Terry Labonte	C&J Energy Ford	143
30	38	36	Dave Blaney	Golden Corral Chevrolet	142
31	7	99	Carl Edwards	Fastenal Ford	142
32	12	42	Juan Pablo Montoya	Target/Kraft Chevrolet	142
33	1	24	Jeff Gordon	DuPont Chevrolet	142
34	40	83	Landon Cassill	Burger King/Dr. Pepper Toyota	141
35	19	48	Jimmie Johnson	Lowe's Chevrolet	61
36	14	39	Ryan Newman	Bass Pro Shops/Tracker Boats Chevrolet	42
37	36	97	Bill Elliott	NEMCO Motorsports Toyota	37
38	43	33	Tony Raines	Little Joe's Autos Chevrolet	32
39	27	30	David Stremme	Stock Car Steel and Aluminum Toyota	30
40	31	78	Regan Smith	Furniture Row Chevrolet	15
41	37	87	Joe Nemechek	AM/FM Energy Wood & Pellet Stoves Toyota	7
42	16	26	Josh Wise*	Morristown Driver's Service Ford	5
43	35	98	Michael McDowell	Curb Records Ford	2

*Sunoco Rookie of the Year Contender

NASCAR Sprint Cup Series
TOP 12
(After 10 Races)

Pos.	Driver	Points	Pos.	Driver	Points
1	GREG BIFFLE	378	7	TONY STEWART	328
2	MATT KENSETH	371	8	JIMMIE JOHNSON	324
3	DALE EARNHARDT JR	369	9	KYLE BUSCH	308
4	DENNY HAMLIN	351	10	CLINT BOWYER	302
5	KEVIN HARVICK	333	11	CARL EDWARDS	300
6	MARTIN TRUEX JR	332	12	BRAD KESELOWSKI	299

Previous spread: Brad Keselowski (No. 2) and Matt Kenseth (No. 17) lead the field through the tri-oval at Talladega.

Opposite page: Casey Mears, holding his daughter Samantha, stands on pit road with his wife Trish and son Hayden.

Above: NASCAR Sprint Cup Series champion Tony Stewart signs autographs in the garage at Talladega.

11

Darlington Raceway
Saturday, May 12, 2012

BOJANGLES' SOUTHERN 500

Back on October 9, 2011, when Jimmie Johnson won at Kansas Speedway and notched the 199th NASCAR Sprint Cup Series race victory for Hendrick Motorsports, no one along pit road would have guessed that it would take seven long months for the venerable car owner to notch number 200.

But for week after week through the rest of the 2011 season and then well into 2012, the Hendrick organization had to postpone any celebration and continue hauling around boxes of special "200th victory" caps from track to track while the mega-team agonized through a mini-slump. That slump was decisively stopped at NASCAR's oldest superspeedway, Darlington Raceway, when Johnson dominated the Bojangles' Southern 500 in his No. 48 Lowe's/Kobalt Tools Chevrolet and led the final 44 laps before winning by 0.781 of a second over Denny Hamlin. Tony Stewart was third, followed by Kyle Busch and Martin Truex Jr.

"We've been awfully close to winning the 200th for him the last month or two," Johnson said after recording his own 56th career victory, which makes the five-time NASCAR Sprint Cup champion responsible for more than a quarter of his car owner's total wins. "My mind goes back to the early days of Hendrick Motorsports, the people that won the early races, worked on the early cars, helped Rick build Hendrick Motorsports to what it is today. I think of Harry Hyde, Tim Richmond, Geoff Bodine, Kenny Schrader – a lot of people over the years that put a lot of time and effort and commitment into this organization."

The first Hendrick victory came on April 29, 1984 when Geoff Bodine won at Martinsville Speedway. Over the next 28 years, 14 other drivers would drive to Victory Lane in Hendrick cars, piling up the wins and championships until reach-

A beautiful southern sunset and a healthy crowd put an exclamation mark on the 63rd running of the Southern 500 at Darlington Raceway.

ing the milestone of 200 wins.

There's something so NASCAR-traditional when you start talking about 200 victories, since that's the all-but-unbreakable all-time record for wins by a driver that was set by "King" Richard Petty in his incomparable career. The fact that Hendrick, a car owner who has generally fielded multiple cars each season, is now reaching 200 is a testament to Petty's greatness.

Petty, a bit surprisingly, only won three races at Darlington, which is precisely the number of Darlington victories in Johnson's resume after taking this race.

Johnson led 134 of the 368 laps, more or less dominating the race. He had to survive two restarts while leading in the late stages of the race, but pulled away from the rest of the field both

times. NASCAR Sprint Cup points leader Greg Biffle won the pole and led 74 laps, second to Johnson, but faded to 12th while his points lead faded to two points over Kenseth.

Hendrick was in the North Carolina mountains at a wedding earlier in the day, but flew to Darlington to catch the final 100 miles and see Johnson drive his team into the history books. Once it was over, Hendrick was mobbed while Johnson pulled the car up to the inside wall and his teammates began pounding on the hood.

"I feel very, very fortunate to go along on this ride," Hendrick said.

"That guy's something," Johnson said. "He said, 'We won 200. Let's get 250.'"

11 | Bojangles' Southern 500

FIN	ST	CAR	DRIVER	SPONSOR	LAPS
1	2	48	Jimmie Johnson	Lowe's / Kobalt Tools Chevrolet	368
2	8	11	Denny Hamlin	Sport Clips Toyota	368
3	17	14	Tony Stewart	Office Depot / MOBIL 1 Chevrolet	368
4	5	18	Kyle Busch	Wrigley Doublemint Toyota	368
5	6	56	Martin Truex Jr	NAPA Auto Parts Toyota	368
6	19	17	Matt Kenseth	Zest Ford	368
7	7	99	Carl Edwards	Ford EcoBoost Fusion Ford	368
8	3	5	Kasey Kahne	Rockwell Tools Chevrolet	368
9	28	9	Marcos Ambrose	DeWalt Ford	368
10	21	20	Joey Logano	The Home Depot Toyota	368
11	26	15	Clint Bowyer	5-hour Energy Toyota	368
12	1	16	Greg Biffle	3M / OH / ES Ford	368
13	14	27	Paul Menard	Menards / Pittsburgh Paints Chevrolet	368
14	9	78	Regan Smith	Furniture Row / CSX Play it Safe Chevrolet	368
15	15	2	Brad Keselowski	Miller Lite Dodge	368
16	23	29	Kevin Harvick	Budweiser Chevrolet	368
17	24	88	Dale Earnhardt Jr	Diet Mountain Dew / National Guard Chevrolet	368
18	10	31	Jeff Burton	BB&T Chevrolet	368
19	13	43	Aric Almirola	Gravely Mower Ford	368
20	18	55	Mark Martin	Aaron's Dream Machine Toyota	368
21	25	51	Kurt Busch	Phoenix Construction Services Chevrolet	368
22	31	13	Casey Mears	GEICO Ford	367
23	4	39	Ryan Newman	WIX Chevrolet	367
24	27	42	Juan Pablo Montoya	Target Chevrolet	366
25	36	38	David Gilliland	A&W All American Food Ford	366
26	20	83	Landon Cassill	Burger King / Dr. Pepper Toyota	366
27	34	36	Dave Blaney	SealWrap.com Chevrolet	365
28	37	34	David Ragan	Peanut Patch / Margaret Holmes Ford	364
29	22	47	Bobby Labonte	Scott Products Toyota	364
30	42	32	Reed Sorenson	Southern Pride Trucking Ford	363
31	38	10	Danica Patrick	GoDaddy.com Chevrolet	362
32	33	73	Travis Kvapil	Burger King / Dr. Pepper Toyota	362
33	16	22	AJ Allmendinger	Shell Pennzoil Dodge	357
34	11	1	Jamie McMurray	Bass Pro Shops / Allstate Chevrolet	345
35	12	24	Jeff Gordon	Drive to End Hunger / AARP Chevrolet	339
36	41	93	David Reutimann	Burger King / Dr. Pepper Toyota	314
37	43	49	J.J. Yeley	America Israel Racing / JPO Absorbents Toyota	132
38	39	74	Cole Whitt	Turn One Racing Chevrolet	35
39	32	30	David Stremme	Inception Motorsports Toyota	32
40	40	87	Joe Nemechek	AM/FM Energy Wood & Pellet Stoves Toyota	27
41	35	52	Mike Skinner	CrusaderStaffing.com Toyota	20
42	29	79	Scott Speed	Team Kyle / KOMA Unwind Ford	20
43	30	26	Josh Wise*	Morristown Drivers Service Ford	19

*Sunoco Rookie of the Year Contender

NASCAR Sprint Cup Series

TOP 12
(After 11 Races)

Pos.	Driver	Points	Pos.	Driver	Points
1	GREG BIFFLE	411	7	TONY STEWART	369
2	MATT KENSETH	409	8	KEVIN HARVICK	361
3	DALE EARNHARDT JR	397	9	KYLE BUSCH	349
4	DENNY HAMLIN	394	10	CARL EDWARDS	337
5	JIMMIE JOHNSON	372	11	CLINT BOWYER	335
6	MARTIN TRUEX JR	372	12	BRAD KESELOWSKI	328

Opposite page: Race winner Jimmie Johnson, his crew chief Chad Knaus and car owner Rick Hendrick celebrate Hendrick's 200th victory as a car owner in the NASCAR Sprint Cup Series.

Above: The famous "Darlington Stripe" stands out on the right side of Aric Almirola's Richard Petty Motorsports No. 43 Gravely Mower Ford.

NON-
POINTS
EVENT
Charlotte Motor Speedway
Saturday, May 19, 2012

NASCAR SPRINT
ALL-STAR RACE

Jimmie Johnson captured the first segment of the NASCAR Sprint All-Star Race at Charlotte Motor Speedway and then used the slight advantage it gave him to speed to victory in the final 10-lap dash to the finish line and win first prize of $1 million.

Johnson led all 10 laps of the final segment to win by 0.841 of a second over Brad Keselowski. Matt Kenseth was third, followed by Kyle Busch and Dale Earnhardt Jr. It was Johnson's third victory in the event, tying a record he now shares with the late Dale Earnhardt and his teammate Jeff Gordon, the only other three-time winners.

The race was run in five segments: four 20-lap runs followed by the final 10-lap sprint. Before the final dash, the winners of the first four segments lined up one through four before a mandatory trip down pit road. Everyone had to at least stop in their pit, so from there it was simply a matter of who got back out on the track first for the final sprint.

Johnson, having won the first segment, was first into the pits before the final run – and first out in his No. 48 Lowe's Patriotic Chevrolet. "Everybody knew if you could win that first segment, you could control the night," Johnson said in the winner's interview. "We were able to do that starting sixth, so it was pretty awesome."

After winning the first segment and securing his first-place ticket into the finals, Johnson dropped back for the other segments, since he gained no advantage by mixing it up with the leaders. Kenseth won the second segment, while Keselowski was in front for the third segment and Earnhardt Jr. captured segment four.

"Well, I can't take the credit for figuring the format out," Johnson said. "I think when the rules came down, every crew chief in the garage area realized the importance of that first

In the Sprint Showdown preceding the NASCAR Sprint All-Star Race, Dale Earnhardt Jr. (No. 88) leads Martin Truex Jr. (No. 56), Jeff Burton (No. 31) and Jamie Mc-Murray (No. 1) on his way to a 2.384-second victory in the qualifying event.

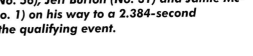

segment. If you won the first segment, it was very easy what you could do. There was just as much importance, not as much, but very close, amount of importance to win the second race. We felt like the winner would come out of the front row, unless these guys got crazy and crashed or something.

"To make your odds work in your favor, being on that front row is key," Johnson said. "First or second segment was the goal to win. We figured starting sixth, winning the second segment was our best chance, but we had such an awesome car, we just went

up there and won the first one."

After winning the race, Johnson and car owner Rick Hendrick celebrated by having Hendrick climb halfway into the driver's window to take a celebratory mini-lap from pit road out to the frontstretch. Hendrick ended up hanging on for dear life, but made it without falling out of the car.

"It's the dumbest thing I've ever done," Hendrick said. "I'm surprised I didn't get called to the [NASCAR] hauler."

NASCAR Sprint All-Star Race

FIN	ST	CAR	DRIVER	SPONSOR	LAPS
1	6	48	Jimmie Johnson	Lowe's Patriotic Chevrolet	90
2	19	2	Brad Keselowski	Miller Lite Dodge	90
3	15	17	Matt Kenseth	Fifth Third Bank Ford	90
4	1	18	Kyle Busch	M&M's Toyota	90
5	21	88	Dale Earnhardt Jr.	Dale Jr. Foundation / National Guard / Diet Mountain Dew Chevrolet	90
6	5	29	Kevin Harvick	Budweiser / Rheem Chevrolet	90
7	18	9	Marcos Ambrose	DeWalt Ford	90
8	17	51	Kurt Busch	Monster Energy Chevrolet	90
9	20	5	Kasey Kahne	Farmers Insurance Chevrolet	90
10	2	39	Ryan Newman	Tornados Chevrolet	90
11	22	22	AJ Allmendinger	Pennzoil Dodge	90
12	10	78	Regan Smith	Furniture Row Racing Chevrolet	90
13	8	24	Jeff Gordon	DuPont Chevrolet	90
14	12	15	Clint Bowyer	5-hour Energy Toyota	90
15	11	21	Trevor Bayne	Good Sam / Camping World Ford	90
16	7	27	Paul Menard	Menards / CertainTeed Chevrolet	90
17	9	14	Tony Stewart	Bass Pro Shops Chevrolet	90
18	14	34	David Ragan	US Shredder Ford	90
19	23	47	Bobby Labonte	Kingsford Toyota	90
20	3	11	Denny Hamlin	FedEx Office Toyota	90
21	16	55	Mark Martin	Aaron's Dream Machine Toyota	90
22	4	16	Greg Biffle	3M / American Red Cross Ford	67
23	13	99	Carl Edwards	Fastenal Ford	25

Opposite page: Race winner Jimmie Johnson (No. 48) and Matt Kenseth (No. 17) lead the field out of the fourth turn toward a green flag.

Above: Jimmie Johnson and his team celebrate his record-tying third victory in the NASCAR Sprint All-Star Race.

12

Charlotte Motor Speedway
Sunday, May 27, 2012

COCA-COLA 600

In the big Hendrick Motorsports party that celebrated the car owner's 200th victory in the NASCAR Sprint Cup Series, all of the drivers who had won races for the team over the years took the stage. Not among them was Kasey Kahne, the first-year Hendrick driver who had wanted to drive for the legendary car owner so bad, he spent the 2011 season in a holding-pattern ride until he could take over the seat of the No. 5 Chevrolet.

Hendrick's attitude about that was to challenge his newest driver, asking him if he was going to win the upcoming Coca-Cola 600 at Charlotte Motor Speedway.

"I hope so," the low-key Kahne had replied.

"Yeah, I don't say too much," Kahne would later recall. "I'd rather just try to perform when it's time."

And perform he did. Two weeks and a day after Jimmie Johnson won Hendrick victory No. 200 at Darlington, Kahne won No. 201 for the legendary owner in a pulling-away victory in the Coca-Cola 600 at Charlotte Motor Speedway. Driving a green-and-white Hendrick Chevrolet sponsored by Quaker State, Kahne won by 4.295 seconds over Denny Hamlin. Kyle Busch was third, followed by Greg Biffle and Brad Keselowski.

"It feels really good," Kahne said in Victory Lane. "It's so special and awesome to drive for Rick and Linda Hendrick."

Kahne averaged 155.687 miles per hour in the fastest Coca-Cola 600 ever. The race was largely trouble-free and slowed by only five minor yellow flags.

It was Kahne's 13th career victory and the third time he's visited Victory Lane in NASCAR's longest race. But it was his first for Hendrick, and that made it extra special.

"It feels good to get a win for Hendrick Motorsports," Kahne said in the winner's interview. "It's something I've been looking forward to, for a year and a half, to drive for Hendrick

Jeff Gordon's gas man fills his No. 24 Drive to End Hunger Chevrolet on pit road at Charlotte Motor Speedway during the Coca-Cola 600.

Motorsports, to be teammates with Jimmie, Dale and Jeff. To put it all together tonight and get the win, it feels good."

While Kahne led 96 laps, including the final 44 trips around the 1.5-mile Charlotte oval, Biffle dominated the first two-third of race, leading a total of 204 laps and holding the point after 100, 200, 300 and 400 miles. But after the sun went down and the track cooled and changed, so did Biffle's Ford. "Kasey got good as the night fell and we seemed to struggle a little bit," Biffle said. "As the speeds picked up and it cooled down, our car was down a little bit harder on the nose and it just kept sliding up the race track."

His fourth-place finish, however, kept him on top of the points standings in the NASCAR Sprint Cup championship, where he has been since the season's third race at Las Vegas in March.

12 | Coca-Cola 600

FIN	ST	CAR	DRIVER	SPONSOR	LAPS
1	7	5	Kasey Kahne	Quaker State Chevrolet	400
2	8	11	Denny Hamlin	FedEx Ground Toyota	400
3	17	18	Kyle Busch	M&M's Red-White-Blue Toyota	400
4	4	16	Greg Biffle	Fastenal Ford	400
5	24	2	Brad Keselowski	Miller Lite Dodge	400
6	12	88	Dale Earnhardt Jr	Nat'l Guard-American Salute/Diet Mtn. Dew Chev	400
7	23	24	Jeff Gordon	Drive to End Hunger Chevrolet	400
8	14	29	Kevin Harvick	Budweiser Folds of Honor Chevrolet	400
9	28	99	Carl Edwards	Fastenal Ford	400
10	20	17	Matt Kenseth	Fastenal Ford	399
11	3	48	Jimmie Johnson	Lowe's Patriotic Chevrolet	399
12	15	56	Martin Truex Jr	NAPA Auto Parts Toyota	399
13	5	15	Clint Bowyer	5-hour Energy Toyota	398
14	16	39	Ryan Newman	U.S. ARMY Chevrolet	398
15	9	27	Paul Menard	Menards/Serta Chevrolet	398
16	1	43	Aric Almirola	U.S. Air Force Ford	398
17	10	78	Regan Smith	Furniture Row Chevrolet	398
18	18	83	Landon Cassill	Burger King Real Fruit Smoothies Toyota	398
19	22	31	Jeff Burton	Wheaties Chevrolet	398
20	29	42	Juan Pablo Montoya	Target Chevrolet	398
21	31	1	Jamie McMurray	Bass Pro Shops/Arctic Cat Chevrolet	397
22	25	13	Casey Mears	GEICO Ford	397
23	19	20	Joey Logano	Dollar General Toyota	397
24	13	21	Trevor Bayne	Motorcraft/Quick Lane Tire & Auto Ctr. Ford	397
25	21	14	Tony Stewart	Office Depot/Mobil 1 Chevrolet	397
26	39	38	David Gilliland	Mod Space Ford	397
27	42	51	Kurt Busch	Phoenix Construction Services Inc. Chevrolet	396
28	26	47	Bobby Labonte	Kingsford Charcoal Toyota	396
29	37	93	Travis Kvapil	Dr. Pepper Toyota	395
30	40	10	Danica Patrick	GoDaddy.com Chevrolet	395
31	41	32	T.J. Bell	Green Smoke Ford	390
32	2	9	Marcos Ambrose	DeWalt Ford	367
33	11	22	AJ Allmendinger	Shell Pennzoil Dodge	361
34	6	55	Mark Martin	Aaron's Armed Forces Foundation Toyota	338
35	30	34	David Ragan	Al's Liners/Scorpion Coatings Ford	281
36	32	98	Michael McDowell	Presbyterian Healthcare Ford	228
37	38	95	Scott Speed	Jordan Truck Sales Ford	136
38	35	30	David Stremme	Inception Motorsports Toyota	86
39	34	33	Stephen Leicht*	Little Joe's Autos/Precon Chevrolet	74
40	36	36	Dave Blaney	SealWrap Chevrolet	54
41	43	87	Joe Nemechek	AM/FM Energy / SWM Toyota	47
42	27	74	Cole Whitt	Turn One Racing Chevrolet	33
43	33	26	Josh Wise*	MDS Transport Ford	15

*Sunoco Rookie of the Year Contender

NASCAR Sprint Cup Series TOP 12
(After 12 Races)

Pos.	Driver	Points	Pos.	Driver	Points
1	GREG BIFFLE	453	7	KEVIN HARVICK	398
2	MATT KENSETH	443	8	KYLE BUSCH	391
3	DENNY HAMLIN	437	9	TONY STEWART	388
4	DALE EARNHARDT JR	435	10	CARL EDWARDS	372
5	JIMMIE JOHNSON	405	11	BRAD KESELOWSKI	368
6	MARTIN TRUEX JR	404	12	CLINT BOWYER	366

Previous spread: A thunderhead rises skyward to the south of turn one at Charlotte Motor Speedway while thunder rises from the track as 43 NASCAR Sprint Cup Series cars road around the 1.5-mile speedway.

Opposite page top: Kasey Kahne celebrates his first victory with Hendrick Motorsports.

Opposite page bottom: Tony Stewart visits with a young NASCAR fan.

Above: The highly acclaimed Marine Band performs during pre-race festivities.

13

Dover International Speedway
Sunday, June 3, 2012

FEDEX 400 BENEFITING AUTISM SPEAKS

No track seems to suit a driver quite the way Dover International Speedway suits Jimmie Johnson, who romped his way around the one-mile, high-banked oval, leading 289 of 400 laps to win his second victory in three races.

Then he romped in Victory Lane, wearing a multi-colored clown wig to promote a sponsor movie: *Madagascar 3: Europe's Most Wanted.*

"God, I love this place!" Johnson said on his radio after taking the checkered flag for his seventh Dover victory in his Hendrick Motorsports No. 48 Lowe's Madagascar Chevrolet".

"You whipped 'em today," crew chief Chad Knaus said. Johnson's seventh win at Dover tied him with NASCAR legends Richard Petty and Bobby Allison for most wins at the Delaware track. He swept the pair of races at Dover in 2002 and 2009 and the FedEx 400 Benefiting Autism Speaks victory set up another chance for him in 2012.

No one else had much to offer at Dover. Kevin Harvick finished second, 2.55 seconds behind Johnson, but never led a lap. Matt Kenseth finished third after leading two laps. Dale Earnhardt Jr. was fourth, leading one lap. And Clint Bowyer finished fifth but never led. No one else in the top 10 led a lap.

Johnson's Hendrick Motorsports teammate Jeff Gordon and pole winner Mark Martin led 60 and 43 laps respectively, but faded to finish 13th and 14th.

The victory concluded a dominating four-week stretch for Hendrick Motorsports that featured victories by Johnson at Darlington and in the NASCAR Sprint All-Star Race at Charlotte Motor Speedway and Kasey Kahne's win there in the Coca-Cola 600.

With crew chief Steve Addington looking on at right, Tony Stewart's crew works furiously to repair his Chevrolet, which was heavily damaged in a 12-car crash on the ninth lap and left him with a 25th-place finish.

"It was just a fun day," Johnson said in the winner's interview. "Clearly we had a fast race car, amazing pit stops. Strategy, when you lead the most laps, sometimes at the end the way the cautions fall it can backfire on the dominant car, and the way cautions fell today, it allowed us to really flex our muscle and bring home the win.

"So proud of the effort," Johnson said, "and, you know, it was a brand-new race car we brought to the track. (The car) had never seen a race track before and rolled off the truck and (was) awesome all weekend long."

The race got off to a rowdy start on lap nine with a 12-car crash on the backstretch that collected Tony Stewart and most of the back of the pack.

Johnson's second 2012 victory set him up well for the Chase for the NASCAR Sprint Cup, but he brushed off talk of a sixth NASCAR Sprint Cup Series championship.

"You know, it's just way too early to talk championship," Johnson said. "I mean, we are doing the things right now that will win one, but we need to do this in September and on. We need to keep the pressure on and roll into September with the same thing going on in order to win a championship."

13 | FedEx 400
Benefiting Autism Speaks

FIN	ST	CAR	DRIVER	SPONSOR	LAPS
1	2	48	Jimmie Johnson	Lowe's Madagascar Chevrolet	400
2	6	29	Kevin Harvick	Jimmy John's Chevrolet	400
3	5	17	Matt Kenseth	Best Buy Ford	400
4	17	88	Dale Earnhardt Jr	AMP Energy/Diet Mtn. Dew/Nat'l Guard Chev	400
5	4	15	Clint Bowyer	5-hour Energy Toyota	400
6	12	43	Aric Almirola	Jani-King / Smithfield Ford	400
7	18	56	Martin Truex Jr	NAPA Auto Parts Toyota	400
8	11	20	Joey Logano	The Home Depot Toyota	400
9	13	5	Kasey Kahne	Hendrickcars.com Chevrolet	400
10	21	9	Marcos Ambrose	Stanley Ford	400
11	7	16	Greg Biffle	3M / Heilind (EMD) Ford	400
12	16	2	Brad Keselowski	Miller Lite Dodge	400
13	14	24	Jeff Gordon	DuPont Chevrolet	400
14	1	55	Mark Martin	Aaron's Dream Machine Toyota	400
15	3	39	Ryan Newman	Quicken Loans Chevrolet	400
16	23	22	AJ Allmendinger	Shell Pennzoil Dodge	400
17	20	27	Paul Menard	Menards / Pittsburgh Paints Chevrolet	400
18	10	11	Denny Hamlin	FedEx Freight / Autism Speaks Toyota	400
19	24	1	Jamie McMurray	Bass Pro Shops / Allstate Chevrolet	400
20	22	47	Bobby Labonte	Scott Products Toyota	399
21	28	34	David Ragan	MHP / 8 hour Alert Ford	398
22	15	31	Jeff Burton	BB&T Chevrolet	364
23	42	93	Travis Kvapil	Burger King / Dr Pepper Toyota	348
24	9	51	Kurt Busch	Phoenix Construction Services Chevrolet	338
25	29	14	Tony Stewart	MOBIL 1 / Office Depot Chevrolet	331
26	19	99	Carl Edwards	SUBWAY Ford	318
27	26	78	Regan Smith	Furniture Row / CSX Play it Safe Chevrolet	306
28	31	42	Juan Pablo Montoya	Target Chevrolet	296
29	8	18	Kyle Busch	M&M's Toyota	202
30	38	32	Reed Sorenson	FAS Lane Racing Ford	124
31	39	10	David Reutimann	Tommy Baldwin Racing Chevrolet	110
32	41	36	Dave Blaney	Tommy Baldwin Racing Chevrolet	65
33	32	30	David Stremme	Inception Motorsports Toyota	63
34	34	49	J.J. Yeley	America Israel Racing / JPO Absorbents Toyota	41
35	37	33	Stephen Leicht*	LittleJoesAutos.com Chevrolet	29
36	36	19	Mike Bliss	Humphrey Smith Racing Toyota	23
37	43	23	Scott Riggs	North Texas Pipe Chevrolet	21
38	27	83	Landon Cassill	Burger King / Dr Pepper Toyota	9
39	35	87	Joe Nemechek	AM/FM Energy Wood & Pellet Stoves Toyota	9
40	30	38	David Gilliland	Autism Speaks Ford	9
41	40	13	Casey Mears	GEICO Ford	8
42	33	98	Michael McDowell	Phil Parsons Racing Ford	8
43	25	79	Scott Speed	Team Kyle / Koma Unwind Ford	8

*Sunoco Rookie of the Year Contender

NASCAR Sprint Cup Series

TOP 12
(After 13 Races)

Pos.	Driver	Points	Pos.	Driver	Points
1	GREG BIFFLE	486	7	KEVIN HARVICK	440
2	MATT KENSETH	485	8	TONY STEWART	407
3	DALE EARNHARDT JR	476	9	KYLE BUSCH	406
4	DENNY HAMLIN	464	10	CLINT BOWYER	405
5	JIMMIE JOHNSON	453	11	BRAD KESELOWSKI	400
6	MARTIN TRUEX JR	441	12	CARL EDWARDS	390

Previous spread: With eventual race winner Jimmie Johnson (No. 48) on his outside, Kevin Harvick (No. 29) leads the field down the frontstretch at the Monster Mile.

Opposite page: Hendrick Motorsports drivers Jimmie Johnson (right) and Dale Earnhardt Jr. chat in the garage at Dover International Speedway during a practice session.

Above: Hendrick Motorsports driver Kasey Kahne finished ninth in the FedEx 400 Benefiting Autism Speaks at Dover.

14

Pocono Raceway
Sunday, June 10, 2012

POCONO 400
PRESENTED BY #NASCAR

Joey Logano's first NASCAR Sprint Cup Series victory at New Hampshire Motor Speedway in 2009 was a rain-shortened affair, and as one might expect, he was more than happy to take the "W." But the sense that it wasn't considered real left an unpleasant aftertaste that lasted for a long time.

A driver would rather win by domination than default; a victory caused merely by the vicissitudes of weather. And the fact it took Logano almost three years to get back to Victory Lane made his win in the Pocono 400 Presented by #NASCAR that much sweeter.

"I didn't stop screaming until I got to Victory Lane," Logano said.

Logano beat Mark Martin to the finish line by 0.997 of a second after bumping him out of the way to take the lead with four laps to go on the 2.5-mile triangular speedway. Tony Stewart finished third, followed by Jimmie Johnson and Denny Hamlin.

Although Logano won the pole and led the most laps – 49 out of 160 – he didn't exactly dominate at the "Tricky Triangle," trading the lead with nine other drivers, five of whom led more than 10 laps.

But his Joe Gibbs Racing No. 20 The Home Depot Toyota was clearly the strongest toward the end, and he appeared to have the race locked up when NASCAR put out the yellow flag for debris in turn two on lap 150. The race resumed with eight laps to go with Martin taking the outside spot on the double-wide restart.

"On every restart, (Martin) was getting a little better, and he got me the last one," Logano said. "I said, 'I'm giving one away here.' I thought about taking the outside (on the final restart), and I thought, 'The bottom has worked every restart

Joey Logano (No. 20) led 49 laps in the Pocono 400 Presented by #NASCAR, including the final four circuits, on his way to his second career victory.

before that.'

"When he got in front of me, I was trying to get right to him, and made a couple mistakes, and he was driving away a little bit and then he made a mistake off of 3, and I was able to have a big run coming to him there. Went into 1 and tried to out-brake him, and he was protecting the bottom. I was trying to stick my nose in there, and we got really close, and I'm not even sure if we touched each other or not, but I know I got him air loose, at least, and was able to slide up underneath him and clear him by the time he got off of 1."

"I'd call that a bump-and-run," Martin said. "It has been accept-able in this racing for a long time. It's not how I would have done it. Certainly, had I had a fast enough car, he would have gotten a re-turn."

For the first time in more than three months, the NASCAR Sprint Cup Series found itself with a new leader atop the points standings, as Matt Kenseth took the top spot from teammate Greg Biffle, taking a 10-point lead over Dale Earnhardt Jr. Kenseth and Earnhardt Jr. finished seventh and eighth in the race. Biffle was 24th, the last driver on the lead lap, and slipped to third in points after holding the top spot for 11 races, stretching back to Las Vegas and the season's third event.

14 | Pocono 400
Presented by #NASCAR

FIN	ST	CAR	DRIVER	SPONSOR	LAPS
1	1	20	Joey Logano	The Home Depot Toyota	160
2	6	55	Mark Martin	Aaron's Dream Machine Toyota	160
3	22	14	Tony Stewart	MOBIL 1 / Office Depot Chevrolet	160
4	24	48	Jimmie Johnson	Lowe's / Kobalt Tools Chevrolet	160
5	5	11	Denny Hamlin	FedEx Express Toyota	160
6	16	15	Clint Bowyer	5-hour Energy Toyota	160
7	14	17	Matt Kenseth	Ford EcoBoost Fusion Ford	160
8	8	88	Dale Earnhardt Jr	National Guard / Diet Mtn. Dew Chevrolet	160
9	3	27	Paul Menard	Menards / Sylvania Chevrolet	160
10	11	1	Jamie McMurray	Banana Boat Chevrolet	160
11	2	99	Carl Edwards	Kellogg's / Cheez-It Ford	160
12	18	39	Ryan Newman	HAAS Automation Chevrolet	160
13	9	9	Marcos Ambrose	DeWalt Ford	160
14	21	29	Kevin Harvick	Rheem Chevrolet	160
15	20	31	Jeff Burton	The Armed Forces Foundation Chevrolet	160
16	7	78	Regan Smith	Furniture Row Chevrolet	160
17	17	42	Juan Pablo Montoya	Target Chevrolet	160
18	31	2	Brad Keselowski	Miller Lite Dodge	160
19	12	24	Jeff Gordon	DuPont Chevrolet	160
20	23	56	Martin Truex Jr	NAPA Auto Parts Toyota	160
21	25	51	David Reutimann	Phoenix Construction Services Chevrolet	160
22	27	47	Bobby Labonte	Bubba Burgers Toyota	160
23	36	38	David Gilliland	ModSpace Motorsports Ford	160
24	13	16	Greg Biffle	3M / Rite Aid / NextCare Ford	160
25	42	10	Dave Blaney	Tommy Baldwin Racing Chevrolet	159
26	37	93	Travis Kvapil	Burger King / Dr Pepper Toyota	159
27	34	34	David Ragan	Taco Bell Ford	159
28	29	43	Aric Almirola	Transportation Impact Ford	158
29	10	5	Kasey Kahne	Farmers Insurance Chevrolet	139
30	4	18	Kyle Busch	M&M's Toyota	76
31	19	22	AJ Allmendinger	Shell Pennzoil Dodge	64
32	40	36	Tony Raines	SealWrap.com Chevrolet	47
33	43	33	Stephen Leicht*	LittleJoesAutos.com Chevrolet	39
34	30	98	Michael McDowell	Presbyterian Healthcare Ford	37
35	26	13	Casey Mears	GEICO Ford	36
36	32	49	J.J. Yeley	America Israel Racing / JPO Absorbents Toyota	33
37	33	87	Joe Nemechek	AM/FM Energy Wood & Pellet Stoves Toyota	30
38	28	19	Mike Bliss	Humphrey Smith Racing Toyota	26
39	39	74	Stacy Compton	Turn One Racing / Country Suites Chevrolet	24
40	38	23	Scott Riggs	North Texas Pipe Chevrolet	19
41	41	32	Reed Sorenson	Herr Foods / Hero Energy Shot Ford	12
42	35	26	Josh Wise*	MDS Transport Ford	12
43	15	83	Landon Cassill	Burger King - Real Fruit Smoothies Toyota	1

*Sunoco Rookie of the Year Contender

Opposite page: Dale Earnhardt Jr.(No. 88) leads eventual race winner Joey Logano (No. 20), Denny Hamlin (No. 11) and others around the "tricky triangle" at Pocono.

Above: Ageless Mark Martin was leading the Pocono 400 with four laps to go when Joey Logano muscled past to take the lead.

NASCAR Sprint Cup Series TOP 12
(After 14 Races)

Pos.	Driver	Points	Pos.	Driver	Points
1	MATT KENSETH	523	7	MARTIN TRUEX JR	465
2	DALE EARNHARDT JR	513	8	TONY STEWART	448
3	GREG BIFFLE	507	9	CLINT BOWYER	443
4	DENNY HAMLIN	504	10	BRAD KESELOWSKI	426
5	JIMMIE JOHNSON	493	11	CARL EDWARDS	423
6	KEVIN HARVICK	470	12	KYLE BUSCH	420

15

Michigan International Speedway
Sunday, June 17, 2012

QUICKEN LOANS 400

An entire nation – Junior Nation – had waited four long years for this, and two additional days on top of that.

At NASCAR speedways from coast to coast from 2008 to 2012, grandstands had erupted in roars time and again as Dale Earnhardt Jr. took the lead, only to settle back down when, at the end of every race, another driver was in Victory Lane.

But after four years, two days and 143 races, finally the long wait was over as Earnhardt Jr. cruised under the checkered flag in front of roaring grandstands at Michigan International Speedway to win the Quicken Loans 400 in his Hendrick Motorsports No. 88 Diet Mountain Dew/The Dark Knight Rises/National Guard Chevrolet after dominating the race.

Earnhardt Jr. was 5.393 seconds ahead of Tony Stewart, who was followed by Matt Kenseth, Greg Biffle and Jimmie Johnson. Since all three NASCAR Sprint Cup Series points leaders finished in the top five, there was no change at the top in the points rankings, with Kenseth leading Earnhardt Jr. and Biffle.

Although Earnhardt Jr. cruised to the win with an uncommonly large margin of victory, no comfort was felt in those last laps by the man in the driver's seat. Even though Junior had won 18 NASCAR Sprint Cup races, he had won only twice since 2005 and had only the lone Michigan victory in 2008 to show for his more than four years driving for car owner Rick Hendrick.

"I was so nervous in the last few laps of that race [here] four years ago, and today, this was the worst. That's the worst feeling riding around there with 15 laps to go wondering what's going to happen or how you were going to lose," he

On a pleasant June afternoon in southern Michigan, Greg Biffle (No. 16) leads the field under the green flag on a restart in the Quicken Loans 400.

said, laughing. "I was just thinking, man, those laps could not go by fast enough. I was like, 'I've got a big lead, I'm going to take it easy....No, I want to run it hard, get it over with.' So I was just in there going crazy, thinking.... And I'm looking all around the race track hoping there's no debris around the next corner. I just knew I was going to come around the next corner and see a piece of metal laying in the race track. I was just waiting on something to happen. So that was terrifying, to be honest with you."

Earnhardt Jr. led 95 of the 200 laps around the two-mile Michigan oval, climbing up from his starting position of 17th to lead for the first time on lap 70. From then on, it was largely his show.

"I was a little nervous when the race started," he said. "The car was not quite where I needed it to be. We were not in too big of trouble. But we needed some adjustments.. . ." He said crew chief Steve Letarte "made the right calls, and the thing took off flying." The victory was a happy one for nearly everyone, because Earnhardt endured his winless streak with seemingly endless stoicism and grace. He slapped hands with countless crewmen on his way to Victory Lane, where he was visited by Jimmie Johnson, Jeff Gordon and other drivers.

"I kept thinking about Steve and the team and how hard we have worked and how we deserved to win, and how we should win, and was hoping it would happen for everybody," Junior said. "You know, that race four years ago was a fuel mileage race, and today we just whooped them really good. So that felt good."

15 | Quicken Loans 400

FIN	ST	CAR	DRIVER	SPONSOR	LAPS
1	17	88	Dale Earnhardt Jr	DietMtnDew/TheDarkKnightRises/NatlGuardChev	200
2	8	14	Tony Stewart	Office Depot/Mobil 1 Chevrolet	200
3	6	17	Matt Kenseth	Ford EcoBoost Ford	200
4	3	16	Greg Biffle	3M/Salute Ford	200
5	10	48	Jimmie Johnson	Lowe's Chevrolet	200
6	28	24	Jeff Gordon	DuPont Chevrolet	200
7	13	15	Clint Bowyer	5-hour Energy Toyota	200
8	21	42	Juan Pablo Montoya	Target Chevrolet	200
9	1	9	Marcos Ambrose	Stanley Ford	200
10	2	29	Kevin Harvick	Budweiser Folds of Honor Chevrolet	200
11	42	99	Carl Edwards	Fastenal Ford	200
12	16	56	Martin Truex Jr	NAPA Auto Parts Toyota	200
13	25	2	Brad Keselowski	Miller Lite Dodge	200
14	19	1	Jamie McMurray	McDonald's Chevrolet	200
15	5	39	Ryan Newman	US ARMY Chevrolet	199
16	31	47	Bobby Labonte	Charter Toyota	199
17	15	43	Aric Almirola	Medallion Ford	199
18	32	83	Landon Cassill	Burger King Toyota	199
19	20	22	AJ Allmendinger	Shell Pennzoil Dodge	199
20	24	13	Casey Mears	Valvoline NEXTGEN Ford	199
21	33	31	Jeff Burton	Caterpillar Chevrolet	199
22	18	27	Paul Menard	Menards/Duracell Chevrolet	199
23	38	34	David Ragan	Front Row Motorsports Ford	199
24	22	33	Austin Dillon	American Ethanol Chevrolet	198
25	36	36	Dave Blaney	Seal Wrap Chevrolet	198
26	39	93	Travis Kvapil	Burger King Toyota	197
27	35	38	David Gilliland	Long John Silver's Ford	197
28	12	78	Regan Smith	Furniture Row Chevrolet	197
29	14	55	Mark Martin	Aaron's Dream Machine Toyota	195
30	26	51	Kurt Busch	Phoenix Construction Services, Inc. Chevrolet	194
31	40	32	Ken Schrader	Federated Auto Parts Ford	193
32	34	18	Kyle Busch	Snickers Toyota	157
33	4	5	Kasey Kahne	Farmers Insurance Chevrolet	151
34	11	11	Denny Hamlin	FedEx Office Toyota	132
35	9	20	Joey Logano	The Home Depot Toyota	125
36	41	10	Tony Raines	Tommy Baldwin Racing Chevrolet	68
37	43	49	J.J. Yeley	America Israel Racing/JPO Absorbents Toyota	67
38	27	98	Michael McDowell	Presbyterian Healthcare Ford	41
39	29	19	Mike Bliss	Humphrey Smith Racing, LLC Toyota	35
40	37	87	Joe Nemechek	AM/FM Energy Wood & Pellet Stoves Toyota	32
41	23	23	Scott Riggs	North TX Pipe Chevrolet	27
42	30	26	Josh Wise*	MDS Transport Ford	9
43	7	21	Trevor Bayne	Motorcraft/Quick Lane Tire & Auto Center Ford	7

*Sunoco Rookie of the Year Contender

NASCAR Sprint Cup Series

TOP 12
(After 15 Races)

Pos.	Driver	Points	Pos.	Driver	Points
1	MATT KENSETH	565	7	MARTIN TRUEX JR	497
2	DALE EARNHARDT JR	561	8	TONY STEWART	491
3	GREG BIFFLE	548	9	CLINT BOWYER	481
4	JIMMIE JOHNSON	532	10	BRAD KESELOWSKI	458
5	DENNY HAMLIN	514	11	CARL EDWARDS	456
6	KEVIN HARVICK	504	12	KYLE BUSCH	432

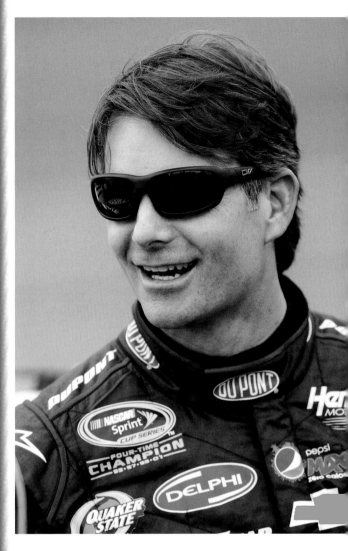

Opposite page: Dale Earnhardt Jr., his girlfriend, Amy Reimann, and the crew of the Hendrick Motorsports No. 88 Diet Mountain Dew/The Dark Knight Rises/National Guard Chevrolet celebrate his first NASCAR Sprint Cup Series win in four years.

Above: Jeff Gordon flashes a wide smile at Michigan International Speedway, where he started 28th in the Quicken Loans 400 but fought his way up to finish sixth.

■ □ ■ ■ ■ ■ **16** ■ ■ ■ ■ ■ ■ ■ ■ ■ ■ ■ ■ ■ ■

Sonoma
Sunday, June 24, 2012

TOYOTA/SAVE MART 350

Every year at the two road races in the NASCAR Sprint Cup Series, the starting line-up features a certain number of road-racing specialists who are not regulars. They often perform well, but almost never beat NASCAR's best, many of whom are just as good as anyone when it comes to turning both left and right.

This year, the fellow who taught the road-course ringers the "how-to," was a dirt-track car slingin' Kansas boy, Clint Bowyer, who led 71 of the 112 laps around the 1.99-mile road course at Sonoma in his Michael Waltrip Racing No. 15 5-hour Energy Toyota before winning a green-white-checkered overtime finish to win the Toyota/Save Mart 350 by 0.829 of a second over Tony Stewart. Kurt Busch was third after a marvelous run in his in his No. 51 Phoenix Construction Services Chevrolet, followed by Brian Vickers, another surprising high finisher, and Jimmie Johnson.

"To have this dirt boy in Victory Lane at this road course is big," Bowyer said. "It is unbelievable to get with a new bunch of people and win races. You have to be with good people and that's what it takes to be successful. Everyone is working very well together. I've had good teammates before but I've never had anything of this magnitude."

It was Bowyer's sixth career victory, but his first since leaving Richard Childress Racing after 2011 to join MWR.

"This victory means a lot to us," added crew chief Brian Pattie. "Clint lost his ride and I lost my job a year ago. I am blessed to be here. Our pace was good and we weren't going to let this one get away from us."

It was a fight to the bitter end, though. Although Bowyer led most of the second half of the race, he usually had someone on his bumper, right to the final turn, when Stewart made a dive-bomb effort into turn 11 in a vain effort to try to

Carl Edwards (No. 99) leads Brad Keselowski (No. 2) and the rest of the field up the hill and through turn two on the 12-turn road course at Sonoma.

at least get to Bowyer's back bumper.

Much of the pressure came from Busch, the defending race winner at Sonoma, but trying yet again to prove himself after a one-race suspension for threatening a reporter kept him from competing at Michigan. Busch led two laps and pestered Bowyer to no end for lap after lap in the later stages of the race, but finally began to fade and was eventually overtaken by Stewart, a two-time winner at the Sonoma, Ca., track.

"It's an amazing day when you can do what we did today," said an emotional Busch. "I'm a little choked up because A, we were in position. B, I was very considerate to Bowyer, who was going for his first win with the new team. And then C, which was most im-

portant, I made a mistake. I got into those tires in turn 11 and for years they have never been bolted down. They were bolted down this time. It bent the right front up and it broke the panhard bar and I'm just glad we brought it home third."

Busch added, "I want to thank (car owner) James Finch, who is at home. He said, 'I don't need that.' I was hoping I could be there and could bring it home for them."

But Bowyer, just as hungry, wasn't about to let the victory go. "This is big for our confidence level – this team," he said. "It's a young organization that's going to be in this sport a long time and I'm proud to be part of it."

FIN	ST	CAR	DRIVER	SPONSOR	LAPS
1	6	15	Clint Bowyer	5-hour Energy Toyota	112
2	24	14	Tony Stewart	Office Depot / MOBIL 1 Chevrolet	112
3	8	51	Kurt Busch	Phoenix Construction Services Chevrolet	112
4	21	55	Brian Vickers	RKMotorsCharlotte.com Toyota	112
5	3	48	Jimmie Johnson	Lowe's Chevrolet	112
6	2	24	Jeff Gordon	Drive to End Hunger Chevrolet	112
7	4	16	Greg Biffle	3M / US Stationary Ford	112
8	1	9	Marcos Ambrose	Stanley Ford	112
9	17	22	AJ Allmendinger	Shell Pennzoil Dodge	112
10	14	20	Joey Logano	The Home Depot Toyota	112
11	35	31	Jeff Burton	Wheaties Chevrolet	112
12	13	2	Brad Keselowski	Miller Lite Dodge	112
13	9	17	Matt Kenseth	Ford EcoBoost Ford	112
14	15	5	Kasey Kahne	Farmers Insurance Chevrolet	112
15	20	13	Casey Mears	GEICO Ford	112
16	26	29	Kevin Harvick	Rheem Chevrolet	112
17	7	18	Kyle Busch	M&M's Toyota	112
18	10	39	Ryan Newman	Quicken Loans/Children's Tumor Foun. Chevrolet	112
19	25	1	Jamie McMurray	McDonald's Chevrolet	112
20	23	27	Paul Menard	Menards / Moen Chevrolet	112
21	11	99	Carl Edwards	Aflac Ford	112
22	5	56	Martin Truex Jr	NAPA Auto Parts Toyota	112
23	19	88	Dale Earnhardt Jr	Diet Mountain Dew/National Guard/7-Eleven Chev	112
24	18	47	Bobby Labonte	Clorox Toyota	111
25	22	95	Scott Speed	Leavine Family Racing Ford	111
26	27	38	David Gilliland	1-800-LoanMart Ford	111
27	29	34	David Ragan	Green 1 High Performance Green Ford	111
28	30	43	Aric Almirola	Medallion Ford	110
29	28	32	Boris Said	HendrickCars.com Ford	110
30	40	26	Josh Wise*	MDS Transport Ford	110
31	42	83	Landon Cassill	Burger King / Dr Pepper Toyota	110
32	31	78	Regan Smith	Furniture Row / Farm American Chevrolet	109
33	38	49	J.J. Yeley	America Israel Racing / JPO Absorbents Toyota	107
34	12	42	Juan Pablo Montoya	Target Chevrolet	107
35	16	11	Denny Hamlin	FedEx Ground Toyota	98
36	39	93	Travis Kvapil	Burger King / Dr Pepper Toyota	92
37	32	36	Dave Blaney	Tommy Baldwin Racing Chevrolet	84
38	41	10	Tomy Drissi	Ice Age Continental Drift Chevrolet	78
39	34	7	Robby Gordon	MAPEI / Save Mart Supermarkets Dodge	73
40	33	98	David Mayhew	Phil Parsons Racing Ford	25
41	43	33	Stephen Leicht*	LittleJoesAutos.com Chevrolet	22
42	37	19	Chris Cook	Humphrey Smith Racing Toyota	13
43	36	87	Joe Nemechek	AM/FM Energy Wood & Pellet Stoves Toyota	1

*Sunoco Rookie of the Year Contender

NASCAR Sprint Cup Series **TOP 12** (After 16 Races)

Pos.	Driver	Points	Pos.	Driver	Points
1	MATT KENSETH	596	7	CLINT BOWYER	529
2	GREG BIFFLE	585	8	DENNY HAMLIN	523
3	DALE EARNHARDT JR	582	9	MARTIN TRUEX JR	520
4	JIMMIE JOHNSON	571	10	BRAD KESELOWSKI	490
5	TONY STEWART	533	11	CARL EDWARDS	479
6	KEVIN HARVICK	532	12	KYLE BUSCH	459

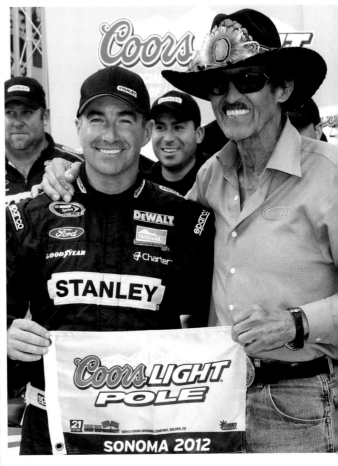

Previous spread: Clint Bowyer (No. 15) gets his Toyota up on two wheels after bouncing off a curb during practice for the Toyota/Save Mart 350.

Opposite page: Ryan Newman adds his autograph in silver to a black racing helmet already full of the signatures of other drivers.

Above: Marcos Ambrose and his car owner, Richard Petty, celebrate Ambrose's second pole position of the season, which he captured with a speed of 95.262 miles per hour.

 17

Kentucky Speedway
Saturday, June 30, 2012

QUAKER STATE 400

B rad Keselowski could not have gotten off to a worse start during the Quaker State 400 weekend at Kentucky Speedway, crashing his Penske Racing No. 2 Miller Lite Dodge on his first lap of practice around the 1.5-mile oval.

But in the stifling heat, his Penske crew transformed his Martinsville short-track car – his backup – into a race winner at Kentucky, giving him a Dodge that led 68 of the 267 laps, including the final 56 trips around the speedway.

Keselowski darted away from the field on a final restart with 48 laps to go and won by a comfortable 4.399 seconds over Kasey Kahne. Denny Hamlin finished third, followed by Dale Earnhardt Jr. and Jeff Gordon.

"What a weekend, man," Keselowski said in Victory Lane. "It started off, we hit the wall on lap one in practice and brought out our backup. This is my Martinsville car from the Chase last year. This ain't the newest car we got, but it sure runs."

Keselowski became the first NASCAR Sprint Cup Series driver to win three races in 2012, and the accomplishment gave him a secure position in the Chase for the NASCAR Sprint Cup. It was the seventh career victory for the 28-year-old Michigan native, enjoying a stellar campaign in his fifth year in the series.

"I tell you what, they put together a back-up car from last year in 100-degree heat in an hour's time – not even an hour," Keselowski said. "It was like 40 minutes. I wish I had a stopwatch for that. Got it on the race track and got to run our laps for practice to make the adjustments we needed to be fast today. And that's what badasses do, and that's what got us to Victory Lane today, and I'm proud of these guys for it. I'm proud of them. Damn proud of them."

After wrecking his primary car on the first lap of practice, Brad Keselowski got busy with his crew and helped prepare his back-up car, which he drove to victory in the race.

"It was probably the toughest weekend as a team that we've ever had up to this point," said crew chief Paul Wolfe. "Not only did we have obviously really high temperatures. But having trouble on the first lap of the race track always sets you back. One thing about all the guys on the Miller Lite team is it seems like we're able to find another level to work when it comes to adversity. I think you see that with the driver as well as you look back to last summer when Bad Brad had a broken foot. And we were able to take that (and win at Pocono and Bristol) and I don't know if he thrives off of that or what, but it seems like when some people might think we're down and out, we're able to find a whole other-level to compete and find ourselves in Victory Lane."

Kyle Busch led a race-high 118 laps, but bounced off the wall coming off one corner and broke a shock absorber. He faded to 10th, but said, "We salvaged a heck of a finish for what all we had to go through."

Kahne found himself in the opposite position, coming on strong in the final laps. He moved through the field up into second, but couldn't get close to Keselowski. "I just hoped he'd run out of gas," said Kahne. "No way I was catching him."

Matt Kenseth's seventh-place finish was good enough to keep him atop the NASCAR Sprint Cup points, holding an 11-point edge over Earnhardt.

17 | Quaker State 400

FIN	ST	CAR	DRIVER	SPONSOR	LAPS
1	8	2	Brad Keselowski	Miller Lite Dodge	267
2	19	5	Kasey Kahne	Quaker State Chevrolet	267
3	3	11	Denny Hamlin	FedEx Express Toyota	267
4	7	88	Dale Earnhardt Jr	Diet Mnt.Dew/National Guard Chevrolet	267
5	9	24	Jeff Gordon	Drive to End Hunger Chevrolet	267
6	1	48	Jimmie Johnson	Lowe's Dover White Chevrolet	267
7	20	17	Matt Kenseth	Fifth Third Bank Ford	267
8	10	56	Martin Truex Jr	NAPA Auto Parts Toyota	267
9	16	22	AJ Allmendinger	Shell Pennzoil Dodge	267
10	2	18	Kyle Busch	M&M's Red-White-Blue Toyota	267
11	4	29	Kevin Harvick	Budweiser Folds of Honor Chevrolet	267
12	15	27	Paul Menard	Menards/Sylvania Chevrolet	267
13	12	9	Marcos Ambrose	Mac Tools Ford	267
14	31	42	Juan Pablo Montoya	Target Chevrolet	267
15	17	1	Jamie McMurray	McDonald's Chevrolet	267
16	6	15	Clint Bowyer	5-hour Energy Toyota	267
17	34	93	Travis Kvapil	Burger King Toyota	267
18	21	13	Casey Mears	Valvoline NextGen Ford	267
19	14	51	Kurt Busch	Phoenix Construction Services, Inc. Chevrolet	267
20	25	99	Carl Edwards	UPS Ford	266
21	11	16	Greg Biffle	American Red Cross Ford	266
22	18	20	Joey Logano	Dollar General Toyota	266
23	38	10	David Reutimann	Outsourcing in the USA@TMone Chevrolet	266
24	29	31	Jeff Burton	Caterpillar Chevrolet	266
25	23	83	Landon Cassill	Burger King Toyota	266
26	13	43	Aric Almirola	Eckrich Ford	266
27	28	47	Bobby Labonte	Scott Products Toyota	265
28	40	38	David Gilliland	Taco Bell Ford	265
29	33	34	David Ragan	Front Row Motorsports Ford	263
30	39	55	Michael Waltrip	Aaron's Dream Machine Toyota	262
31	41	32	Ken Schrader	Federated Auto Parts Ford	262
32	22	14	Tony Stewart	Office Depot/Mobil 1 Chevrolet	231
33	26	78	Regan Smith	Furniture Row Chevrolet	209
34	5	39	Ryan Newman	Tornados Chevrolet	208
35	42	36	Dave Blaney	SealWrap Chevrolet	144
36	32	30	David Stremme	Inception Motorsports Toyota	71
37	30	26	Josh Wise*	MDS Transport Ford	60
38	35	98	Michael McDowell	Presbyterian Health Care Ford	58
39	24	95	Scott Speed	Leavine Family Racing Ford	55
40	27	87	Joe Nemechek	AM/FM Energy Wood & Pellet Stoves Toyota	52
41	43	33	Stephen Leicht*	LittleJoesAuto.com Chevrolet	47
42	37	19	Mike Bliss	Humphrey Smith Racing, LLC Toyota	18
43	36	23	Scott Riggs	North TX Pipe Chevrolet	12

*Sunoco Rookie of the Year Contender

NASCAR Sprint Cup Series **TOP 12** (After 17 Races)

Pos.	Driver	Points	Pos.	Driver	Points
1	MATT KENSETH	633	7	CLINT BOWYER	557
2	DALE EARNHARDT JR	622	8	MARTIN TRUEX JR	556
3	JIMMIE JOHNSON	610	9	TONY STEWART	545
4	GREG BIFFLE	608	10	BRAD KESELOWSKI	537
5	DENNY HAMLIN	565	11	CARL EDWARDS	503
6	KEVIN HARVICK	565	12	KYLE BUSCH	495

Previous spread: The NASCAR Sprint Cup Series field is lined up on pit road before the Quaker State 400 at Kentucky Speedway.

Opposite page: Kyle Busch (No. 18), who led a race-high 118 laps, stays in front as Jimmie Johnson (No. 48) battles inside of Brad Keselowski (No. 2) on the 1.5-mile Kentucky oval.

Above: Miss Sprint Cup Kim Coon celebrates in Victory Lane with the winning Penske Racing team.

18

COKE ZERO 400
POWERED BY COCA-COLA

Tony Stewart brought his summer magic back to Daytona International Speedway, winning his fourth Coke Zero 400 Powered by Coca-Cola with a dramatic last-lap pass. But his success in the July classic just made him hunger that much more for similar results in the Daytona 500.

"I wish I could trade a couple of these races in for just one Sunday race in February," said Stewart, winner of 18 races at Daytona, second only to the late Dale Earnhardt's 34 victories.

Stewart managed to make it past the Roush Fenway Racing tandem of Greg Biffle and Matt Kenseth on the backstretch of the final lap in his Stewart-Haas Racing No. 14 MOBIL 1/Office Depot Chevrolet and captured the race as the caution flag flew for a 15-car accident in turn four. Jeff Burton was second, followed by Kenseth, Joey Logano and Ryan Newman.

Stewart qualified second, but had to start at the back of the field after his time was thrown out when his car failed post-qualifying inspection. So he was content to let Biffle and Kenseth dominate most of the show with Biffle leading 35 laps and the Daytona 500 champ a race-high 89 laps.

Stewart didn't lead until lap 131 of the 160-lap race, and was in front for 21 straight laps, until the Kenseth-Biffle team pushed past on lap 152. Two laps later, however, the caution flew for a significant wreck – a 14-car crash in the tri-oval of the 2.5-mile speedway. That kept the caution out until lap 158, setting up a two-lap finale.

On the final lap, the field sailed through turns one and two side-by-side, with Kenseth leading and Biffle behind him. But on the outside, Stewart was getting a huge push from Kasey Kahne. Suddenly, Burton's car, with teammate Kevin Harvick

Roush Fenway Racing teammates Greg Biffle (No. 16) and Matt Kenseth (No. 17) lead the field past the start-finish line and the main grandstands at Daytona International Speedway.

on his bumper, got loose, and he slid up and disturbed Kahne's run, breaking his draft with Stewart.

But Stewart still had all the momentum Kahne had given him, and managed to get past both Biffle and Kenseth on the backstretch, breaking their draft in the process before pulling down in front of them. It was free sailing after that, with the turn four crash taking out Biffle and many drivers behind him.

"I don't even remember what happened that last lap," said the defending NASCAR Sprint Cup Series champion. "I just got in that second lane and just tried to get the No. 17 (Kenseth) and No. 16 (Biffle) pulled apart. Once we got them pulled apart it gave us a run on the outside."

Said Kenseth, "I was going to make sure I kept Greg with me and did a really good job for a lap and a quarter. We were locked on there. Somehow Greg got off me, but I think Tony was separated, as well."

The victory was the third of the season for Stewart, making him a virtual lock for a spot in the Chase for the NASCAR Sprint Cup. And it was the 47th of his career, moving him ahead of Buck Baker into 14th place on the list of all-time NASCAR race winners, and just behind another old-timer, Herb Thomas, who won 48 races in the 1950s.

Kenseth remained at the top of the NASCAR Sprint Cup points standings, with a 25-point edge over Dale Earnhardt Jr. as the series headed to New Hampshire.

18 | Coke Zero 400
Powered by Coca-Cola

FIN	ST	CAR	DRIVER	SPONSOR	LAPS
1	42	14	Tony Stewart	MOBIL 1 / Office Depot Chevrolet	160
2	20	31	Jeff Burton	Wheaties Chevrolet	160
3	1	17	Matt Kenseth	Zest Ford	160
4	19	20	Joey Logano	Dollar General Toyota	160
5	2	39	Ryan Newman	Aspen Dental Chevrolet	160
6	12	99	Carl Edwards	Subway Ford	160
7	3	5	Kasey Kahne	HendrickCars.com Chevrolet	160
8	9	2	Brad Keselowski	Miller Lite Dodge	160
9	28	55	Michael Waltrip	Aaron's Dream Machine Toyota	160
10	41	47	Bobby Labonte	Kingsford Charcoal Toyota	160
11	39	10	David Reutimann	CarportEmpire.com/TMone.com Call Ctrs Chev	160
12	5	24	Jeff Gordon	PepsiMax Chevrolet	160
13	30	1	Jamie McMurray	Bass Pro Shops / NRA Museum Chevrolet	160
14	13	27	Paul Menard	Quaker State / Menards Chevrolet	160
15	24	88	Dale Earnhardt Jr	Ntl Guard-An American Salute/Diet Mtn Dew Chev	160
16	40	93	Travis Kvapil	Burger King / Dr Pepper Toyota	160
17	18	56	Martin Truex Jr	NAPA Batteries Toyota	160
18	7	13	Casey Mears	GEICO Ford	160
19	17	43	Aric Almirola	U.S. Air Force Ford	160
20	34	32	Terry Labonte	C & J Energy Services Ford	160
21	4	16	Greg Biffle	3M Ford	160
22	33	36	Dave Blaney	Golden Corral Chevrolet	160
23	11	29	Kevin Harvick	Budweiser Folds of Honor Chevrolet	159
24	22	18	Kyle Busch	Interstate Batteries Toyota	159
25	23	11	Denny Hamlin	FedEx Office Toyota	156
26	27	34	David Ragan	MHP 8-hour Alert Ford	154
27	15	21	Trevor Bayne	Motorcraft / Quick Lane Tire & Auto Center Ford	152
28	14	42	Juan Pablo Montoya	Target Chevrolet	152
29	29	15	Clint Bowyer	5-hour Energy Toyota	152
30	10	9	Marcos Ambrose	DeWalt Ford	152
31	32	38	David Gilliland	Glory Foods Ford	152
32	38	83	Landon Cassill	Burger King / Dr Pepper Toyota	151
33	8	22	Sam Hornish Jr	Shell Pennzoil Dodge	149
34	25	78	Regan Smith	Furniture Row / Farm American Chevrolet	133
35	35	51	Kurt Busch	Phoenix Construction Services Chevrolet	132
36	16	48	Jimmie Johnson	Lowe's Chevrolet	123
37	6	50	Bill Elliott	Walmart Chevrolet	123
38	31	26	Josh Wise*	MDS Transport Ford	47
39	26	30	David Stremme	Stock Car Steel and Aluminum Toyota	25
40	43	49	J.J. Yeley	Robinson-Blakeney Racing Toyota	16
41	36	87	Joe Nemechek	AM/FM Energy Wood & Pellet Stoves Toyota	10
42	37	33	Stephen Leicht*	LittleJoesAutos.com Chevrolet	4
43	21	98	Michael McDowell	Phil Parsons Racing Ford	3

*Sunoco Rookie of the Year Contender

NASCAR Sprint Cup Series TOP 12
(After 18 Races)

Pos.	Driver	Points	Pos.	Driver	Points
1	MATT KENSETH	676	7	DENNY HAMLIN	584
2	DALE EARNHARDT JR	651	8	MARTIN TRUEX JR	584
3	GREG BIFFLE	632	9	BRAD KESELOWSKI	573
4	JIMMIE JOHNSON	618	10	CLINT BOWYER	572
5	TONY STEWART	592	11	CARL EDWARDS	541
6	KEVIN HARVICK	586	12	KYLE BUSCH	516

Previous spread: Three-wide racing is routine at Daytona International Speedway. Here, Ryan Newman (No. 39) has a half-car length edge over Clint Bowyer (No. 15) and Matt Kenseth (No. 17), who is trailed by Greg Biffle (No. 16). Jamie McMurray (No. 1) and Paul Menard (No. 27) are in the mix.

Opposite page: Dale Earnhardt Jr.'s battered No. 88 National Guard - An American Salute/Diet Mountain Dew Chevrolet sits smoking on the apron after wrecking with 14 others cars on the last lap of the race.

Above: Tony Stewart celebrates his third victory of the season and his fourth win in the Coke Zero 400 Powered by Coca-Cola at Daytona International Speedway.

19

New Hampshire Motor Speedway
Sunday, July 15, 2012

LENOX INDUSTRIAL TOOLS 301

One team's mistake became the key ingredient in the winning formula for another team as Kasey Kahne took advantage of a miscommunication between Denny Hamlin and his crew chief to scoot away to victory in the LENOX Industrial Tools 301 at New Hampshire Motor Speedway.

Kahne led the final 66 laps in his Hendrick Motorsports No. 5 Farmers Insurance Chevrolet and held off Hamlin's furious charge back to the front to win by 2.738 seconds, or about 20 car lengths. Clint Bowyer had another strong run to finish third, followed by Dale Earnhardt Jr. and Brad Keselowski.

"We ran in the top five the whole race, but Denny was obviously the best car," Kahne said in Victory Lane. "We had a great Farmers Insurance Chevrolet and we just had to battle hard throughout the whole race. We did it. We had good pit strategy, got the track position, and we were able to lead those final laps there. I was definitely focused on the lapped cars I was going by and how I could clear them quick. So I was paying attention to where he was, but I felt pretty good about the lead we had."

Pole winner Kyle Busch had dominated the first part of the race, leading 72 laps, but a pit road speeding penalty coupled with pit mistakes crippled his effort and left him with a 16th-place finish. Hamlin took over, led 150 laps, and had the race well in control when a yellow flag flew for oil on the track on lap 235.

Moments before the stop, Hamlin called on the radio for "tires" and complained about his handling. Crew chief Darian Grubb was planning for a two-tire stop, which was the recommended strategy. Because it was so difficult to pass on the 1.058-mile oval, maintaining track position was of paramount

Eyes wide open, Ryan Newman sits in his car while parked in the garage during practice at New Hampshire Motor Speedway.

117

importance. But after hearing Hamlin's complaints, Grubb decided to switch to a four-tire stop, and since Kahne and nearly everyone else took two, Hamlin dropped from the lead to 14th place for the restart.

Kahne, meanwhile, inherited the top spot and darted out to a wide lead after the green flag fell. By the time Hamlin clawed his way back through the field to take over second place, he was more than three seconds behind Kahne with less than 25 laps to catch him.

With 10 laps to go, Hamlin had made up about half the distance, but was still a second and a half behind Kahne. With five laps to go, Hamlin was still trailing by 15 car lengths. And when Hamlin dove into turn three too hard with less than a lap to go and drifted up almost to the wall, it was over.

"I just didn't have enough there at the end and it's all we could do," said Hamlin. "We made our bed by taking those four tires. Darian wanted to take two, but I told him I just needed tires and that was it. He took it that I needed four tires. It was just a little miscommunication that turned into a second-place finish. You never know what could have happened on that last restart if we were taking two. The 5 (Kahne) still may have been better, you never know. We obviously had a great car there at the end and made it interesting, at least for the fans."

NASCAR Sprint Cup Series points leader Matt Kenseth finished 13th and saw his lead shrink to 16 points over Dale Earnhardt Jr.

19 | LENOX Industrial Tools 301

FIN	ST	CAR	DRIVER	SPONSOR	LAPS
1	2	5	Kasey Kahne	Farmers Insurance Chevrolet	301
2	3	11	Denny Hamlin	FedEx Freight Toyota	301
3	5	15	Clint Bowyer	5-hour Energy Toyota	301
4	9	88	Dale Earnhardt Jr	National Guard / Diet Mountain Dew Chevrolet	301
5	22	2	Brad Keselowski	Miller Lite Dodge	301
6	8	24	Jeff Gordon	DuPont Chevrolet	301
7	7	48	Jimmie Johnson	Lowe's Chevrolet	301
8	12	29	Kevin Harvick	Rheem Chevrolet	301
9	11	16	Greg Biffle	3M / WB Mason / Post-it Ford	301
10	6	39	Ryan Newman	ARMY ROTC Chevrolet	301
11	4	56	Martin Truex Jr	NAPA Auto Parts Toyota	301
12	10	14	Tony Stewart	MOBIL 1 / Office Depot Chevrolet	301
13	27	17	Matt Kenseth	NESN Ford	301
14	16	20	Joey Logano	The Home Depot Toyota	301
15	15	55	Brian Vickers	MyClassicGarage.com / Aaron's Toyota	301
16	1	18	Kyle Busch	Interstate Batteries Toyota	301
17	13	27	Paul Menard	Menards / Duracell Chevrolet	301
18	21	99	Carl Edwards	Fastenal / LENOX Ford	301
19	20	9	Marcos Ambrose	DeWalt Ford	301
20	28	1	Jamie McMurray	Bass Pro Shops / Allstate Chevrolet	300
21	25	31	Jeff Burton	Caterpillar Chevrolet	300
22	24	22	Sam Hornish Jr	Shell Pennzoil / AAA Dodge	300
23	18	47	Bobby Labonte	Luke & Associates Toyota	300
24	14	51	Kurt Busch	Phoenix Construction Services Chevrolet	299
25	31	42	Juan Pablo Montoya	Degree Chevrolet	299
26	17	78	Regan Smith	Furniture Row / Farm American Chevrolet	298
27	39	38	David Gilliland	Taco Bell Ford	298
28	23	43	Aric Almirola	Medallion Financial Ford	298
29	29	83	Landon Cassill	Burger King / Dr Pepper Toyota	297
30	30	93	Travis Kvapil	Burger King / Dr Pepper Toyota	297
31	37	32	Ken Schrader	Federated Auto Parts Ford	294
32	43	33	Stephen Leicht*	LittleJoesAutos.com Chevrolet	293
33	26	10	David Reutimann	Mohawk Northeast Chevrolet	229
34	19	34	David Ragan	Front Row Motorsports Ford	139
35	40	30	David Stremme	Inception Motorsports Toyota	101
36	33	13	Casey Mears	GEICO Ford	91
37	32	26	Josh Wise*	MDS Transport Ford	82
38	34	87	Joe Nemechek	AM/FM Energy Wood & Pellet Stoves Toyota	71
39	35	36	Dave Blaney	Tommy Baldwin Racing Chevrolet	68
40	36	98	Michael McDowell	Phil Parsons Racing Ford	63
41	41	23	Scott Riggs	North Texas Pipe Chevrolet	32
42	42	79	Kelly Bires	Team Kyle / Bestway Disposal Ford	19
43	38	49	J.J. Yeley	Robinson-Blakeney Racing Toyota	4

*Sunoco Rookie of the Year Contender

 NASCAR Sprint Cup Series **TOP 12** (After 19 Races)

Pos.	Driver	Points	Pos.	Driver	Points
1	MATT KENSETH	707	7	TONY STEWART	618
2	DALE EARNHARDT JR	691	8	MARTIN TRUEX JR	617
3	GREG BIFFLE	667	9	CLINT BOWYER	614
4	JIMMIE JOHNSON	656	10	BRAD KESELOWSKI	613
5 -	DENNY HAMLIN	628	11	CARL EDWARDS	567
6	KEVIN HARVICK	622	12	KASEY KAHNE	547

Opposite page top: Sam Hornish Jr. and Jeff Burton wave to the crowd during a parade lap before the race at New Hampshire.

Opposite page bottom: Ryan Newman (No. 39) leads Brad Keselowski (No. 2) and Denny Hamlin (No. 11) down the frontstretch of the 1.058-mile oval.

Above: A prize New England lobster was part of the booty for Kasey Kahne after winning the LENOX Industrial Tools 301 at New Hampshire Motor Speedway.

20

Indianapolis Motor Speedway
Sunday, July 29, 2012

CROWN ROYAL PRESENTS THE CURTISS SHAVER 400 AT THE BRICKYARD POWERED BY BIG MACHINE RECORDS

You can count on one hand the number of four-time winners at Indianapolis Motor Speedway, and Jimmie Johnson added his name to that elite list with a dominating victory in the Crown Royal Presents the Curtiss Shaver 400 at the Brickyard Powered by Big Machine Records.

Johnson led 99 of the 160 laps around the 2.5-mile speedway in his Hendrick Motorsports No. 48 Lowe's/Kobalt Tools Chevrolet and took the checkered flag with a fat 4.758-second lead over Kyle Busch. Greg Biffle was third, followed by Dale Earnhardt Jr. and Jeff Gordon.

The victory allowed Johnson to join Hendrick Motorsports teammate Jeff Gordon as the only NASCAR drivers to win four Brickyard races at the Indianapolis track, which was built in 1909 and was the first race track to be called a speedway. A.J. Foyt, Al Unser and Rick Mears, who was Johnson's racing idol when he was young, each have won the Indianapolis 500 four times. Formula One ace Michael Schumacher won the U.S. Grand Prix five times when it was run on Indy's road course. Johnson won his first Brickyard 400 in 2006 and added victories in 2008 and 2009.

"Wow, man that victory lap to go around the track is something special," Johnson said in Victory Lane. "To come here and win is a huge honor, then to have four wins. . . I'm at a loss for words."

Johnson appeared to have the race well in hand when a yellow flag flew with 34 laps to go for Jeff Burton's flat tire, bringing the leaders to the pits.

While Johnson and others took four tires, Biffle took only two tires and shot out of the pits in first place. The race resumed with 31 laps to go and Biffle managed to stay in front for a couple of laps, but Johnson got by him on the

Jimmie Johnson (No. 48) leads the field into the first turn at Indianapolis Motor Speedway on his way to a dominating victory in the 400-mile summer classic at the Brickyard.

frontstretch with 29 laps to go.

The race was slowed a final time with 26 laps to go when Joey Logano spun in turn one, collecting NASCAR Sprint Cup Series points leader Matt Kenseth, Bobby Labonte and Trevor Bayne in the process. But for this restart, Johnson now had the lead, and he moved out ahead as soon as the green flag fell.

"This fourth, I'm able to join racing legends, my heroes, people I've looked up to my entire life, so to join them is a huge, huge honor," Johnson said. "I knew second or third lap yesterday on the track that we were going to have an awfully good chance at winning. That confidence that I had helped us through practice yesterday. There were a couple moments where maybe an adjustment didn't work and we lost a little pace, but I just had a feeling, and I just knew we were going to be fine."

Kenseth's crash left him with a DNF and a 35th-place finish, dropping him out of the points lead for the first time in six races. Earnhardt Jr., on the strength of his strong finish at Indy, took the points lead for the first time in 2012, holding a 14-point margin over Kenseth.

20 | Crown Royal Presents The Curtiss Shaver 400 Powered By Big Machine Records

FIN	ST	CAR	DRIVER	SPONSOR	LAPS
1	6	48	Jimmie Johnson	Lowe's/Kobalt Tools Chevrolet	160
2	7	18	Kyle Busch	M&M's Toyota	160
3	5	16	Greg Biffle	3M Ford	160
4	20	88	Dale Earnhardt Jr	AMP Energy/National Guard Chevrolet	160
5	9	24	Jeff Gordon	Drive to End Hunger Chevrolet	160
6	1	11	Denny Hamlin	FedEx Express Toyota	160
7	11	39	Ryan Newman	Quicken Loans Chevrolet	160
8	17	56	Martin Truex Jr	NAPA Auto Parts Toyota	160
9	22	2	Brad Keselowski	Miller Lite Dodge	160
10	28	14	Tony Stewart	Mobil 1/Office Depot Chevrolet	160
11	19	55	Mark Martin	Aaron's Dream Machine Toyota	160
12	15	5	Kasey Kahne	Farmers Insurance Chevrolet	160
13	27	29	Kevin Harvick	Jimmy John's Chevrolet	160
14	8	27	Paul Menard	Menards/Nibco Chevrolet	160
15	33	15	Clint Bowyer	5-hour Energy Toyota	160
16	24	22	Sam Hornish Jr	Shell Pennzoil Dodge	160
17	18	21	Trevor Bayne	Motorcraft/Quick Lane Tire & Auto Center Ford	160
18	14	78	Regan Smith	Furniture Row/Farm American Chevrolet	160
19	4	43	Aric Almirola	Eckrich Ford	160
20	23	9	Marcos Ambrose	DeWalt Ford	160
21	12	42	Juan Pablo Montoya	Target Chevrolet	160
22	16	1	Jamie McMurray	Bass Pro Shops/Tracker Chevrolet	160
23	32	36	Dave Blaney	SealWrap Chevrolet	160
24	26	30	David Stremme	Inception Motorsports Toyota	160
25	38	83	Landon Cassill	Burger King Toyota	160
26	29	47	Bobby Labonte	Scott Products Toyota	160
27	31	38	David Gilliland	Big Machine Records Ford	160
28	36	34	David Ragan	Scorpion Coatings/Al's Liners Ford	160
29	2	99	Carl Edwards	Fastenal Ford	156
30	42	32	Ken Schrader	Special Operations For America.org Ford	156
31	37	33	Stephen Leicht*	LittleJoesAuto.com Chevrolet	154
32	21	31	Jeff Burton	Rain-X Chevrolet	151
33	3	20	Joey Logano	Dollar General Toyota	144
34	25	13	Casey Mears	GEICO Ford	137
35	10	17	Matt Kenseth	Fifth Third Bank Ford	132
36	13	51	Kurt Busch	Hendrickcars.com Chevrolet	126
37	30	93	Travis Kvapil	Burger King Toyota	40
38	34	95	Scott Speed	Leavine Family Racing Ford	23
39	41	10	J.J. Yeley	Tommy Baldwin Racing Chevrolet	20
40	35	26	Josh Wise*	Taco Bell Chevrolet	19
41	40	23	Scott Riggs	North Texas Pipe Chevrolet	14
42	39	79	Mike Skinner	Koma Unwind Ford	11
43	43	19	Mike Bliss	Humphrey-Smith Racing LLC Toyota	5

*Sunoco Rookie of the Year Contender

NASCAR Sprint Cup Series TOP 12
(After 20 Races)

Pos.	Driver	Points	Pos.	Driver	Points
1	DALE EARNHARDT JR	731	7	MARTIN TRUEX JR	653
2	MATT KENSETH	717	8	TONY STEWART	652
3	GREG BIFFLE	709	9	BRAD KESELOWSKI	649
4	JIMMIE JOHNSON	704	10	CLINT BOWYER	643
5	DENNY HAMLIN	667	11	KYLE BUSCH	588
6	KEVIN HARVICK	653	12	CARL EDWARDS	582

Previous spread: The pace car leads the field through the speedway's first turn.

Opposite page top: Joe Gibbs Racing teammates Kyle Busch and Denny Hamlin chat on pit road.

Opposite page bottom: Dale Earnhardt Jr's crew snaps off a four-tire pit stop during the race.

Above: Jimmie Johnson, wife Chandra and daughter Genevieve celebrate his fourth victory at the Brickyard.

21

Pocono Raceway
Sunday, August 5, 2012

PENNSYLVANIA 400

Victory number 86 wasn't the most elegant or spectacular in Jeff Gordon's NASCAR career, but he surely was more grateful for this one than many, despite winning by default in the rain-shortened Pennsylvania 400 at Pocono Raceway.

"I tell you what, the way our year has gone, we'll definitely take it like this," Gordon said while waiting for the official call from NASCAR. Although he led only eight of the scheduled 160 laps, he was in front in his Hendrick Motorsports No. 24 Drive to End Hunger Chevrolet when the skies opened up and the race was called after 98 laps.

Trailing Gordon at the end were Kasey Kahne, Martin Truex Jr., Brad Keselowski and Tony Stewart.

The start of the race was delayed almost two hours by rain, but the intermittent showers gave way to sunshine for a good portion of the afternoon. As the skies again grew dark over the Pocono mountains, everyone knew there was a good chance that the restart after Kurt Busch's accident in turn two on lap 87 would settle the race.

Jimmie Johnson had dominated until then, leading a race-high 44 laps. But as the field dove into turn one, Johnson's Chevy slid up the track and hit Matt Kenseth's Ford. Kenseth spun and collected three other cars, In the mayhem, Gordon powered past all of them and took the lead as the yellow flag flew again. The race was stopped seven laps later as the skies opened up.

"Man, I've never seen the seas part quite like that before like they did going down into one," Gordon said, laughing. "I got a great restart and was able to dive to the inside in front of Kasey and I saw the 48 (Johnson) get sideways and it just took them all out. And I was like, "Wow.'

"And then I was thinking about the (next) restart and what

Juan Pablo Montoya (No. 42) leads Martin Truex Jr. (No. 56) and the rest of the field through a turn at Pocono Raceway during the Pennsylvania 400.

we were going to do. I didn't want to have the same thing happen to us that happened to the 48. And it started raining. I tell you what, with all the things that have gone wrong for us this year, I'm hoping that this is the one that makes up for it all.

"I know that you don't want to win them quite like this, but we've earned it because of all the things that we've done this year," he said. "We've been in position to win races. And we were at the right place at the right time. We just needed some things to go our way and boy did they go our way today."

Despite mechanical problems and a 32nd–place finish, Dale Earnhardt Jr. held onto the NASCAR Sprint Cup Series points lead, mainly because Kenseth's crash also gave him a sub-par, 23rd-place finish. Earnhardt Jr. left Pocono with a five-point lead over Kenseth.

21 | Pennsylvania 400

FIN	ST	CAR	DRIVER	SPONSOR	LAPS
1	27	24	Jeff Gordon	Drive to End Hunger Chevrolet	98
2	4	5	Kasey Kahne	Farmers Insurance Chevrolet	98
3	15	56	Martin Truex Jr	NAPA Auto Parts Toyota	98
4	31	2	Brad Keselowski	Miller Lite Dodge	98
5	28	14	Tony Stewart	Office Depot Back to School Chevrolet	98
6	9	39	Ryan Newman	HAAS Automation / Quicken Loans Chevrolet	98
7	17	99	Carl Edwards	Fastenal Ford	98
8	19	15	Clint Bowyer	5-hour Energy Toyota	98
9	11	78	Regan Smith	Furniture Row / Farm American Chevrolet	98
10	5	9	Marcos Ambrose	Stanley Ford	98
11	3	27	Paul Menard	Menards / Serta Chevrolet	98
12	18	55	Mark Martin	Aaron's Dream Machine Toyota	98
13	14	20	Joey Logano	The Home Depot Toyota	98
14	10	48	Jimmie Johnson	Lowe's Chevrolet	98
15	12	16	Greg Biffle	3M Ford	98
16	21	29	Kevin Harvick	Budweiser Chevrolet	98
17	16	1	Jamie McMurray	Bass Pro Shops / Allstate Chevrolet	98
18	13	43	Aric Almirola	Automotive Lift Institute Ford	98
19	25	22	Sam Hornish Jr	Shell Pennzoil Dodge	98
20	1	42	Juan Pablo Montoya	Target Chevrolet	98
21	26	38	David Gilliland	ModSpace Motorsports Ford	98
22	23	31	Jeff Burton	Enersys / Odyssey Battery Chevrolet	98
23	7	17	Matt Kenseth	Zest Ford	98
24	24	10	David Reutimann	TMone.com Chevrolet	97
25	37	93	Travis Kvapil	Burger King / Dr Pepper Toyota	97
26	22	83	Landon Cassill	Burger King / Dr Pepper Toyota	97
27	39	47	Bobby Labonte	Scott Products Toyota	96
28	32	34	David Ragan	Taco Bell Ford	96
29	2	11	Denny Hamlin	FedEx Ground Toyota	90
30	6	51	Kurt Busch	Phoenix Construction Services Chevrolet	84
31	41	32	Jason White	Zaxby's Ford	81
32	8	88	Dale Earnhardt Jr	Diet Mtn. Dew / AMP Energy / Nat'l Guard Chev	80
33	20	18	Kyle Busch	M&M's Toyota	74
34	36	30	David Stremme	Inception Motorsports Toyota	43
35	29	13	Casey Mears	GEICO Ford	40
36	38	87	Joe Nemechek	AM/FM Energy Wood & Pellet Stoves Toyota	37
37	34	26	Josh Wise*	MDS Transport Ford	34
38	42	36	Tony Raines	@Tmone / CRM Hiring Veterans Chevrolet	31
39	30	19	Mike Bliss	Plinker Tactical Toyota	29
40	35	37	J.J. Yeley	Max Q Motorsports Chevrolet	27
41	43	98	Mike Skinner	TRAQM.com Ford	26
42	40	91	Reed Sorenson	Plinker Tactical Toyota	10
43	33	23	Scott Riggs	North Texas Pipe Chevrolet	9

*Sunoco Rookie of the Year Contender

NASCAR Sprint Cup Series

TOP 12
(After 21 Races)

Pos.	Driver	Points	Pos.	Driver	Points
1	DALE EARNHARDT JR	744	7	BRAD KESELOWSKI	690
2	MATT KENSETH	739	8	DENNY HAMLIN	683
3	GREG BIFFLE	738	9	KEVIN HARVICK	681
4	JIMMIE JOHNSON	736	10	CLINT BOWYER	679
5	MARTIN TRUEX JR	694	11	KASEY KAHNE	622
6	TONY STEWART	691	12	CARL EDWARDS	619

Opposite page: Jeff Gordon's Hendrick Motorsports crew crank out a fast four-tire pit stop as they help him on his way to his 86th career victory.

Above: Jeff Gordon and his daughter Ella enjoy a moment on pit road before the race.

22

FINGER LAKES 355
AT THE GLEN

Oil on any race track is a recipe for disaster, but to Marcos Ambrose and Brad Keselowski, it was just one more challenge during a wild, fender-banging duel on the last lap of the Finger Lakes 355 at the Glen.

Ambrose screeched across the finish line in his Richard Petty Motorsports No. 9 Stanley Ford 0.571 of a second ahead of Keselowski. Jimmie Johnson was third, followed by Clint Bowyer and Sam Hornish Jr.

"It just feels so good to be back in Victory Lane," Ambrose said after his second career victory and second straight win in this road race on The Glen's historic 2.45-mile, seven-turn track. "It just feel so good. This year is pure joy. It's a great day. It's just awesome fun and that's the way racing should be."

This finish was as entertaining as it gets, unless you're Kyle Busch, who was the big victim of a circuit-wide oil slick laid down by Bobby Labonte's sputtering Toyota at the end of the race. Busch had the race well in hand, but got into the oil going through turn one on the last lap and while desperately trying to recover, was tapped by Keselowski and spun into the fence. Busch recovered quickly to finish seventh, but what he really needed at this point in the season was a victory.

"I thought Kyle got loose first on some oil (in turn one), so you can't blame Brad for hitting Kyle," Ambrose said. "The guy was sliding across the track, he was gonna spin out and Brad finished him off. I'm like, 'Man, there's one, I've got one more to go.' I went up over the hill there and I thought I was gonna hit the fence and kept it off the wall and then we get down to the chicane and I'm like, 'Well, I'm just gonna follow Brad because he'll see the oil before I do and I might be able to save myself,' and I went straight off the track with him. That wasn't a good plan. . ."

Juan Pablo Montoya (No. 42) dives into the first turn inside of Kyle Busch (No. 18) as the rest of the field thunders toward the corner behind them.

Both cars slid through the grass coming out of the Inner Loop and fishtailed through the sweeping turn nine. As they fought to keep control coming out of the turn, Ambrose's car tapped Keselowski's, and then the Australian driver managed to get by. Ambrose went way wide through turn six, but stayed ahead of Keselowski as both cars half slid through the final turn.

"It was absolutely chaos at the end," said Ambrose, who led eight of the 90 laps. "I had really burned off the brakes. I couldn't figure out where (the oil) was coming from. It was just absolutely crazy."

"Busch slipped up big in turn one," said Keselowski, who nonetheless took to Twitter after the race to say he was sorry for getting into him. "There was nothing I could do. It was just one big giant oil slick underneath his car. We all checked up and Marcos was right on my bumper. We all just about spun out."

NASCAR Sprint Cup Series points leader Dale Earnhardt Jr. struggled to a 28th-place finish and dropped to fourth in the points as Jimmie Johnson surged to the top by virtue of his third-place finish. Johnson left Watkins Glen with a one-point lead over Greg Biffle and two points ahead of Matt Kenseth. Earnhardt Jr. was 17 points behind.

22 | Finger Lakes 355 at the Glen

FIN	ST	CAR	DRIVER	SPONSOR	LAPS
1	5	9	Marcos Ambrose	Stanley Ford	90
2	4	2	Brad Keselowski	Miller Lite Dodge	90
3	3	48	Jimmie Johnson	Lowe's Cortez Silver Chevrolet	90
4	8	15	Clint Bowyer	5-hour Energy Toyota	90
5	17	22	Sam Hornish Jr	Shell Pennzoil Dodge	90
6	15	16	Greg Biffle	3M Ford	90
7	2	18	Kyle Busch	M&M's Toyota	90
8	24	17	Matt Kenseth	Ford EcoBoost Ford	90
9	13	78	Regan Smith	Furniture Row/Farm American Chevrolet	90
10	9	56	Martin Truex Jr	NAPA Auto Parts Toyota	90
11	6	39	Ryan Newman	U.S. ARMY Chevrolet	90
12	22	27	Paul Menard	Menards/Rheem Chevrolet	90
13	20	5	Kasey Kahne	Farmers Insurance Chevrolet	90
14	18	99	Carl Edwards	Fastenal Ford	90
15	19	29	Kevin Harvick	Budweiser Chevrolet	90
16	30	13	Casey Mears	GEICO Ford	90
17	21	95	Scott Speed	TWD Ford	90
18	29	43	Aric Almirola	Smithfield Ford	90
19	7	14	Tony Stewart	Office Depot/Mobil 1 Chevrolet	90
20	34	38	David Gilliland	Mod Space Ford	90
21	12	24	Jeff Gordon	Drive to End Hunger Chevrolet	90
22	32	34	David Ragan	Scorpion Coatings/Al's Liners Ford	90
23	35	83	Landon Cassill	Burger King/Dr. Pepper Toyota	90
24	42	93	Travis Kvapil	Burger King/Dr. Pepper Toyota	90
25	25	32	Boris Said	Hendrickcars.com Ford	90
26	39	33	Stephen Leicht*	LittleJoesAuto.com Chevrolet	90
27	26	47	Bobby Labonte	Miller Welders/Freightliner Toyota	90
28	16	88	Dale Earnhardt Jr	National Guard/Diet Mountain Dew Chevrolet	89
29	36	87	Joe Nemechek	Genny Light/AM/FM Energy Toyota	88
30	28	31	Jeff Burton	Caterpillar Chevrolet	84
31	27	51	Kurt Busch	Phoenix Construction Services Inc. Chevrolet	81
32	14	20	Joey Logano	The Home Depot Toyota	71
33	1	42	Juan Pablo Montoya	Target Chevrolet	63
34	23	11	Denny Hamlin	FedEx Freight Toyota	57
35	41	49	Jason Leffler	America Israel Racing Toyota	42
36	31	36	Dave Blaney	Tommy Baldwin Racing Chevrolet	41
37	11	98	Michael McDowell	TRAQM Ford	30
38	38	26	Josh Wise*	MDS Transport Ford	25
39	10	1	Jamie McMurray	McDonald's Chevrolet	24
40	37	10	J.J. Yeley	Tommy Baldwin Racing Chevrolet	15
41	40	19	Chris Cook	Plinker Tactical Toyota	5
42	43	30	Patrick Long	Inception Motorsports Toyota	2
43	33	55	Brian Vickers	MyClassicGarage.com Toyota	0

*Sunoco Rookie of the Year Contender

NASCAR Sprint Cup Series TOP 12
(After 22 Races)

Pos.	Driver	Points	Pos.	Driver	Points
1	JIMMIE JOHNSON	777	7	CLINT BOWYER	719
2	GREG BIFFLE	776	8	TONY STEWART	716
3	MATT KENSETH	775	9	KEVIN HARVICK	710
4	DALE EARNHARDT JR	760	10	DENNY HAMLIN	693
5	BRAD KESELOWSKI	733	11	KASEY KAHNE	653
6	MARTIN TRUEX JR	728	12	CARL EDWARDS	650

Previous spread: Marcos Ambrose (No. 9) celebrates his victory with a crowd-pleasing burn out.

Opposite page: Tony Stewart (No. 14) spins off the final turn on his way to crashing into the inside wall. He recovered to finish on the lead lap in 19th place.

Above: Kyle Busch and wife Samantha stroll down pit road at Watkins Glen International.

23

Michigan International Speedway
Sunday, August 19, 2012

PURE MICHIGAN 400

With 10 laps to go in the Pure Michigan 400 at Michigan International Speedway, Jimmie Johnson had passed Brad Keselowski for the lead and was cruising toward his fourth victory of the year in his Hendrick Motorsports No. 48 Lowe's Chevrolet, intent on making a statement of his strength for the coming Chase for the NASCAR Sprint Cup.

With five laps to go, it all ended quite suddenly. The engine troubles that had crippled Jeff Gordon and also put Hendrick engine customer Tony Stewart out of the race on the ultra-fast, two-mile tri-oval rose up and took Johnson out as well, relegating him to a 27th-place finish and his fourth DNF of the season.

Through the engine smoke came Greg Biffle in his Roush Fenway Racing No. 16 3M Ford to grab the victory, flying under the checkered flag 0.416 of a second ahead of Keselowski. Kasey Kahne was third, followed by Dale Earnhardt Jr. and Marcos Ambrose.

Biffle said he thought he could have caught Johnson even if his engine hadn't failed.

"It was going to be a great race no matter what," Biffle said. "I felt like I could catch him, but we'll never know. Passing him might have been a different story. But I certainly think that with seven to go, I probably could have pulled up close to him."

Johnson's reaction was pretty much limited to an anguished cry over his radio as his tachometer needle plunged toward zero. "You've got to be kidding me!' he wailed. Then, moments later, in glum and leaden recognition, he added, "That's it. It's dead."

Although already safely in the Chase for the NASCAR Sprint Cup by virtue of his three victories, Johnson was par-

Pole winner Mark Martin's car (No. 55) suffered significant damage when it slammed into the end of the pit wall, putting him out of the race.

ticularly upset by the loss and hurriedly left the track, uncharacteristically avoiding media interviews.

"It's a valve spring" that failed in at least two of the Hendrick engines, said Jeff Gordon, who finished 28th, one spot behind Johnson. "I think that's the same thing that happened to the No. 14 (Tony Stewart) earlier. It's something that when you come to Michigan and you turn these kinds of sustained rpms on this fast of a track, it's always of concern here. And that bit us. This is a tough place on engines."

Johnson had been leading the NASCAR Sprint Cup points coming to Michigan; he departed in fourth place. The new points leader was Biffle, who had been atop the points for 11 straight races earlier in the season. Matt Kenseth, who finished 17th in the race, took over second in points, 20 behind Biffle.

Biffle's lead in the points, as well as the win, his second of the season, ensured his spot in the Chase for the NASCAR Sprint Cup. "Well, I know that a lot of people don't expect us to win the championship; don't expect us to compete for the title," he said. "I don't care what they say or who they want to talk about or what they talk about. We will be a factor when it comes down to Homestead, I promise you that."

23 | Pure Michigan 400

FIN	ST	CAR	DRIVER	SPONSOR	LAPS
1	13	16	Greg Biffle	3M Ford	201
2	19	2	Brad Keselowski	Miller Lite Dodge	201
3	5	5	Kasey Kahne	Farmers Insurance Chevrolet	201
4	22	88	Dale Earnhardt Jr	National Guard / Diet Mountain Dew Chevrolet	201
5	8	9	Marcos Ambrose	Stanley Ford	201
6	2	99	Carl Edwards	Geek Squad Ford	201
7	12	15	Clint Bowyer	5-hour Energy Toyota	201
8	15	39	Ryan Newman	WIX Chevrolet	201
9	10	27	Paul Menard	Menards / Pittsburgh Paints Chevrolet	201
10	7	56	Martin Truex Jr	NAPA Auto Parts Toyota	201
11	21	11	Denny Hamlin	FedEx Office Toyota	201
12	17	22	Sam Hornish Jr	Shell Pennzoil Dodge	201
13	23	18	Kyle Busch	Interstate Batteries Toyota	201
14	24	1	Jamie McMurray	Bass Pro Shops / Mercury Chevrolet	201
15	30	93	Travis Kvapil	Burger King / Dr Pepper Toyota	201
16	20	29	Kevin Harvick	Jimmy John's Chevrolet	201
17	4	17	Matt Kenseth	Fifth Third Bank Ford	201
18	36	38	David Gilliland	Taco Bell Ford	201
19	32	31	Jeff Burton	Wheaties Chevrolet	201
20	41	43	Aric Almirola	Eckrich Ford	201
21	39	10	David Reutimann	TMone.com Chevrolet	200
22	28	47	Bobby Labonte	Clorox Toyota	199
23	37	34	David Ragan	Long John Silver's Ford	199
24	6	21	Trevor Bayne	Motorcraft / Quick Lane Tire & Auto Center Ford	199
25	9	83	Landon Cassill	Burger King / Dr Pepper Toyota	198
26	25	42	Juan Pablo Montoya	Target Chevrolet	197
27	3	48	Jimmie Johnson	Lowe's Chevrolet	195
28	11	24	Jeff Gordon	Drive to End Hunger / AARP Chevrolet	167
29	18	78	Regan Smith	Furniture Row / Farm American Chevrolet	154
30	26	51	Kurt Busch	Hendrickcars.com Chevrolet	135
31	16	20	Joey Logano	The Home Depot Toyota	132
32	14	14	Tony Stewart	MOBIL 1 / Office Depot Chevrolet	109
33	40	32	T.J. Bell	Southern Pride Trucking / U.S. Chrome Ford	108
34	31	30	David Stremme	Inception Motorsports Toyota	72
35	1	55	Mark Martin	Aaron's Dream Machine Toyota	64
36	35	87	Joe Nemechek	AM/FM Energy Wood & Pellet Stoves Toyota	38
37	29	13	Casey Mears	GEICO Ford	36
38	42	36	Dave Blaney	Tommy Baldwin Racing Chevrolet	34
39	43	98	Mike Skinner	Phil Parsons Racing Ford	25
40	34	26	Josh Wise*	MDS Transport Ford	21
41	38	23	Scott Riggs	North Texas Pipe Chevrolet	20
42	27	91	Reed Sorenson	Plinker Tactical Toyota	15
43	33	19	Jason Leffler	Plinker Tactical Ford	14

*Sunoco Rookie of the Year Contender

NASCAR Sprint Cup Series TOP 12
(After 23 Races)

Pos.	Driver	Points	Pos.	Driver	Points
1	GREG BIFFLE	823	7	CLINT BOWYER	757
2	MATT KENSETH	803	8	KEVIN HARVICK	738
3	DALE EARNHARDT JR	801	9	TONY STEWART	728
4	JIMMIE JOHNSON	795	10	DENNY HAMLIN	727
5	BRAD KESELOWSKI	776	11	KASEY KAHNE	694
6	MARTIN TRUEX JR	763	12	CARL EDWARDS	689

Opposite page top: A tight formation of World War II fighters performs the flyover before the race.

Opposite page bottom: Jimmie Johnson (No. 48) is on the inside of Brad Keselowski (No. 2) for a restart in the Pure Michigan 400.

Above: Greg Biffle celebrates his second victory of the 2012 season in Victory Lane at Michigan.

24

IRWIN TOOLS NIGHT RACE

He had won 19 other times in the NASCAR Sprint Cup Series, but it was clear from the moment Denny Hamlin emerged from his Joe Gibbs Racing No. 11 FedEx Ground Toyota that his victory in the IRWIN Tools Night Race at the revamped Bristol Motor Speedway was as big as any of the previous triumphs.

"My biggest win, this is just such a great feeling," Hamlin said, a huge smile coursing his face in Victory Lane. "This is just a big win. I don't know how else to explain it other than it's the night race at Bristol."

Hamlin led the final 39 laps to win by a rather comfortable 1.103 seconds over Jimmie Johnson, who was trailed by Jeff Gordon, part-timer Brian Vickers, in only his sixth NASCAR Sprint Cup race of the season, and Marcos Ambrose.

Thirteen different drivers led the race, trading the top spot 22 times, but the most dramatic was Hamlin's pass of Carl Edwards on lap 462 of the 500-lap race, giving him a lead he never relinquished.

And just as that pass cemented Hamlin's place in the Chase for the NASCAR Sprint Cup, giving him his third victory of 2012, it seemed to doom Edwards's chances. Edwards was hanging onto the lead with a wing and a prayer anyway, having skipped a pit stop entirely to get there. Indeed, he was doomed not only to fail to win, but even to score a decent finish when the pit strategy backfired. He ran out of fuel and finished 22nd, four laps down.

But Edwards seemed plenty strong with 50 laps to go as he fiercely held onto the lead in the high groove at Bristol, which was the place to be at the reconfigured half-mile, high-banked oval.

The only chance Hamlin had was to dive low below Edwards and slide up in front of him. This he did, tapping Ed-

---

Pole winner Casey Mears (No. 13) and Brad Keselowski (No. 2) lead the 43-car field just before the start of the IRWIN Tools Night Race.

wards a bit in the process. And after he squeezed in front of Edwards, the Ford driver made sure Hamlin knew he was there with a stiff kick to the back bumper. But that was it – the pass was done – and Hamlin checked out as the final laps ran green.

"You did what you had to do," Hamlin said. "The only thing you could do was slide in front of somebody. You still had the old Bristol – it's still one line and you had to knock someone out of the way to make them move."

"It's all you can do is gamble like that," Edwards said. "If we would have pitted when we should have pitted, we were gonna run 10th or 15th anyway. I made the decision to stay out, which in hindsight that was the wrong decision because we probably would have finished better than we are right now, but I wanted a chance to win the race. You don't get those opportunities very often, so I had to take it."

Vickers put on quite a show in his Michael Waltrip Racing Toyota, leading a lap while on his way to a remarkable third top-five finish in only six races in 2012. He finished fifth at Bristol in the spring and fourth at Sonoma. "I gave it all I could, but it wasn't enough," Vickers said. "I'm still really happy with fourth place. Obviously pleased, but not satisfied. I'd

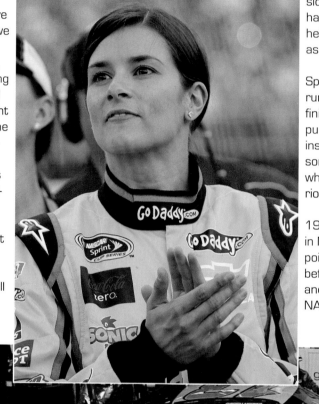

loved to have won this thing and I think we had a shot at it."

Track officials did some grinding on the cement surface to try to make it more like the close-quarters Bristol of old, and it seemed to do the trick. There were 13 yellow flags for 87 laps, and while not close to the Bristol record, that was far more than in the most recent races. The highlight of the night, by far, was a two-car tangle between Tony Stewart and Matt Kenseth while both battled for the lead, leaving them both crashed along the inside wall. In a dramatic, angry, two-handed heave, Stewart bounced his helmet off the front end of Kenseth's car as the crowd roared.

Danica Patrick made her NASCAR Sprint Cup debut at Bristol and she was running credibly and looking at a top-20 finish until Regan Smith unceremoniously punted her, sending her crashing into the inside wall and out of the race. She did some serious finger pointing at Smith when he passed by during the caution period, but kept her helmet in her hand.

Although Greg Biffle struggled to a 19th-place finish, he maintained the lead in NASCAR Sprint Cup points by 11 points over Johnson with only two races before the end of the regular campaign and the beginning of the Chase for the NASCAR Sprint Cup.

24 | IRWIN Tools Night Race

FIN	ST	CAR	DRIVER	SPONSOR	LAPS
1	8	11	Denny Hamlin	FedEx Ground Toyota	500
2	37	48	Jimmie Johnson	Lowe's Dover White Chevrolet	500
3	11	24	Jeff Gordon	FarmVille/Drive to End Hunger Chevrolet	500
4	22	55	Brian Vickers	MyClassicGarage.com Toyota	500
5	9	9	Marcos Ambrose	DeWalt Ford	500
6	10	18	Kyle Busch	M&M's Toyota	500
7	23	15	Clint Bowyer	5-hour Energy Toyota	500
8	4	20	Joey Logano	Dollar General Toyota	500
9	12	5	Kasey Kahne	Hendrickcars.com Chevrolet	500
10	7	27	Paul Menard	Menards/Schrock Chevrolet	500
11	15	56	Martin Truex Jr	NAPA Auto Parts Toyota	500
12	16	88	Dale Earnhardt Jr	Diet Mountain Dew/National Guard Chevrolet	500
13	28	42	Juan Pablo Montoya	Target Chevrolet	500
14	36	47	Bobby Labonte	Bush's Beans Toyota	500
15	13	29	Kevin Harvick	Rheem Chevrolet	500
16	14	78	Regan Smith	Furniture Row/Farm American Chevrolet	500
17	26	1	Jamie McMurray	Bass Pro Shops/Allstate Chevrolet	500
18	41	93	Travis Kvapil	Burger King/Dr. Pepper Toyota	500
19	3	16	Greg Biffle	3M/Bondo Ford	500
20	18	38	David Gilliland	Taco Bell Ford	500
21	1	13	Casey Mears	GEICO Ford	499
22	27	99	Carl Edwards	Fastenal Ford	496
23	30	98	Michael McDowell	K-Love/Curb Records Ford	496
24	33	83	Landon Cassill	Burger King/Dr. Pepper Toyota	490
25	17	17	Matt Kenseth	Valvoline NextGen Ford	486
26	25	36	Dave Blaney	Seal Wrap Chevrolet	476
27	21	14	Tony Stewart	Mobil 1/Office Depot Chevrolet	471
28	20	51	Kurt Busch	Phoenix Construction Chevrolet	440
29	43	10	Danica Patrick	Go Daddy Racing Chevrolet	434
30	2	2	Brad Keselowski	Miller Lite Dodge	434
31	39	49	Jason Leffler	America Israel Racing Toyota	417
32	24	34	David Ragan	Glory Foods Ford	409
33	6	31	Jeff Burton	Caterpillar Chevrolet	360
34	29	22	Sam Hornish Jr	Shell Pennzoil Dodge	343
35	5	43	Aric Almirola	Goody's Ford	235
36	19	39	Ryan Newman	Outback Steakhouse Chevrolet	189
37	31	30	David Stremme	Inception Motorsports Toyota	159
38	32	26	Josh Wise*	MDS Transport Ford	150
39	40	87	Joe Nemechek	AM/FM Energy/AC General Toyota	130
40	38	33	Stephen Leicht*	LittleJoesAuto.com Chevrolet	56
41	35	23	Scott Riggs	North Texas Pipe Chevrolet	20
42	42	32	Ken Schrader	Federated Auto Parts Ford	9
43	34	19	Mike Bliss	Plinker Tactical Toyota	6

*Sunoco Rookie of the Year Contender

NASCAR Sprint Cup Series TOP 12
(After 24 Races)

Pos.	Driver	Points	Pos.	Driver	Points
1	GREG BIFFLE	849	7	BRAD KESELOWSKI	790
2	JIMMIE JOHNSON	838	8	DENNY HAMLIN	774
3	DALE EARNHARDT JR	834	9	KEVIN HARVICK	767
4	MATT KENSETH	823	10	TONY STEWART	746
5	MARTIN TRUEX JR	797	11	KASEY KAHNE	730
6	CLINT BOWYER	794	12	CARL EDWARDS	712

Previous spread: The excitement was back at Bristol Motor Speedway, shown here in its full glory in a panoramic photo taken during the race.

Opposite page top: Danica Patrick applauds during pre-race ceremonies.

Opposite page bottom: A traffic jam sorts itself out on pit road during the race.

Above: Denny Hamlin's face shows how big his win was in the IRWIN Tools Night Race at Bristol Motor Speedway.

25

Atlanta Motor Speedway
Sunday, September 2, 2012

ADVOCARE 500

Martin Truex Jr. was ready to celebrate his contract extension with Michael Waltrip Racing in Victory Lane at Atlanta Motor Speedway with his first win in five years, but fate had other plans in the AdvoCare 500.

With five laps to go and Truex holding a comfortable lead but low on gas, Jamie McMurray blew a tire, smacked the wall, littered the frontstretch with debris and brought out a yellow flag that changed everything.

Truex and the other leaders came to the pits for gas and at least a couple of fresh tires to have better grip on the super-fast, 1.5-mile oval for the green-white-checkered over-time finish to come. But as it turned out, it was in the pits where the battle was won. Denny Hamlin won the contest there, taking two tires and gas and emerging a half-car length ahead of Truex.

And it was all but over as Hamlin darted ahead in his Joe Gibbs Racing No. 11 Sport Clips Toyota on the restart as Truex fell back after spinning his tires when he hit the gas. Jeff Gordon made a valiant stab at Hamlin in the final two turns, but couldn't make anything happen, and Hamlin crossed the line 0.378 of a second ahead of the Chevy driver. Brad Keselowski finished third, followed by Truex and Kevin Harvick.

It was Hamlin's second victory in a row, and his season-leading fourth of the year, and it gave him a huge boost as the NASCAR Sprint Cup Series hurtled toward the Chase for the NASCAR Sprint Cup, with only a single race remaining be-fore the 10-race playoff.

"This was one I wanted real bad," Hamlin said in Victory Lane. "Last week was a big one, no doubt about it. But I've been really good here at Atlanta the last year and not won. Our car faded a little bit, but the pit crew won me the race.

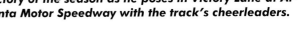

Denny Hamlin holds up four fingers to signify his fourth victory of the season as he poses in Victory Lane at At-lanta Motor Speedway with the track's cheerleaders.

That's what a championship team is all about – to have all those pieces of the puzzle put together. And this year I think we have it all."

Gordon, meanwhile, was almost desperate for a win, mired as he was at 14th place in the points. A win at Atlanta would have given him two for the year and all but secured a Wild Card spot in the Chase.

"I got everything I could ask for," Gordon said afterwards. "I got the restart I wanted, got to the outside and was just too tight and Denny was good there. But he made a mistake off of two and I got a run on him and made a bad decision. I should have just run into the back of him going into three and moved him up the race track and we would have been sitting in Victory Lane right now and counting another win. This Chase is too important for me to be in it and not to make a move like that. I wouldn't have wanted to wreck him, but I would have liked to have that one over again."

As the series headed to Richmond for the final contest before the Chase, Greg Biffle still sat atop the points, as he had after 14 of the year's races. He was a lock for the Chase, as were all top nine in points. Also locked in was Tony Stewart, in

10th, good either by points or with a Wild Card spot. That left Gordon and seven others – Kasey Kahne, Kyle Busch, Marcos Ambrose, Ryan Newman, Joey Logano, Carl Edwards and Paul Menard – to fight for the two spots still up for grabs in the Chase.

"We've got a lot of pressure on us, so we're going to be going there guns loaded and ready to do battle," Gordon said. "I mean, just like what we did tonight. We're just going to fight all the way to that last lap."

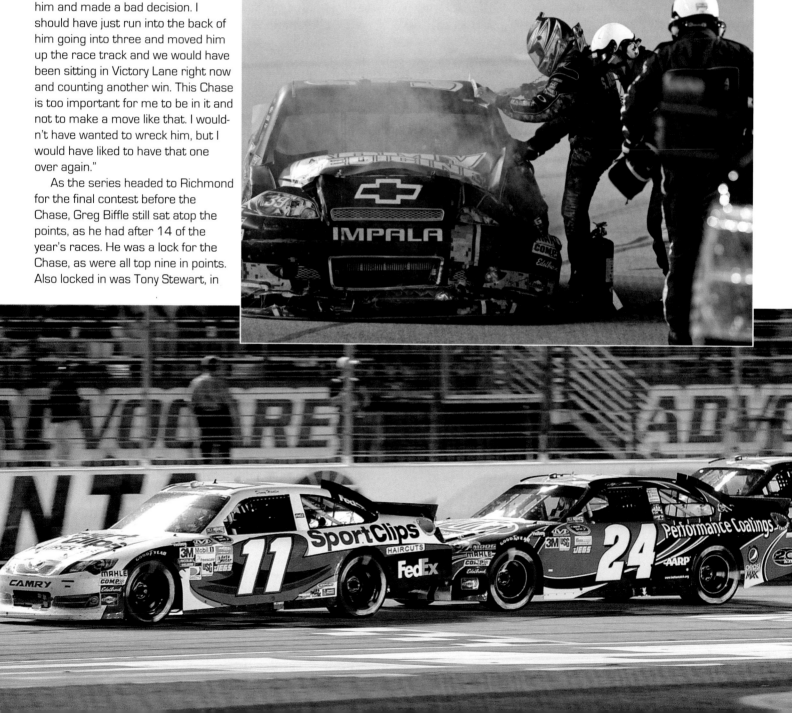

25 | AdvoCare 500

FIN	ST	CAR	DRIVER	SPONSOR	LAPS
1	7	11	Denny Hamlin	Sport Clips Toyota	327
2	5	24	Jeff Gordon	DuPont Chevrolet	327
3	21	2	Brad Keselowski	Miller Lite Dodge	327
4	28	56	Martin Truex Jr	NAPA Shocks Toyota	327
5	24	29	Kevin Harvick	Rheem Chevrolet	327
6	3	18	Kyle Busch	Wrigley / Doublemint Toyota	327
7	35	88	Dale Earnhardt Jr	National Guard / Diet Mountain Dew Chevrolet	327
8	18	27	Paul Menard	Quaker State / Menards Chevrolet	327
9	4	17	Matt Kenseth	Ford Eco Boost Ford	327
10	6	55	Mark Martin	Aaron's Dream Machine Toyota	327
11	15	22	Sam Hornish Jr	Shell Pennzoil Dodge	327
12	26	31	Jeff Burton	Caterpillar Chevrolet	327
13	16	51	Kurt Busch	Hendrickcars.com Chevrolet	327
14	27	78	Regan Smith	Furniture Row / Farm American Chevrolet	327
15	2	16	Greg Biffle	3M / Manheim Auctions Ford	327
16	32	21	Trevor Bayne	Good Sam / Camping World Ford	327
17	10	9	Marcos Ambrose	DeWalt Ford	327
18	9	20	Joey Logano	The Home Depot Toyota	327
19	25	47	Bobby Labonte	Kingsford Toyota	327
20	40	83	Landon Cassill	Burger King Toyota	326
21	33	42	Juan Pablo Montoya	Target Chevrolet	326
22	1	14	Tony Stewart	Office Depot / Mobil 1 Chevrolet	326
23	11	5	Kasey Kahne	Hendrickcars.com Chevrolet	325
24	20	1	Jamie McMurray	Bass Pro Shops / Tracker Boats Chevrolet	325
25	22	36	Dave Blaney	Tommy Baldwin Racing Chevrolet	324
26	41	93	Travis Kvapil	Dr Pepper / Burger King Toyota	324
27	30	15	Clint Bowyer	5-hour Energy Toyota	324
28	14	34	David Ragan	Glory Foods Ford	323
29	23	10	Danica Patrick	GoDaddy.com Chevrolet	321
30	42	32	T.J. Bell	Greensmoke Ford	319
31	29	38	David Gilliland	House - Autry Ford	298
32	13	43	Aric Almirola	AdvoCare Ford	297
33	19	13	Casey Mears	GEICO Ford	291
34	8	48	Jimmie Johnson	Lowe's / Kobalt Tools Chevrolet	269
35	17	39	Ryan Newman	ARMY Medicine Chevrolet	268
36	12	99	Carl Edwards	Subway Ford	264
37	36	95	Scott Speed	Jordan Truck Sales Ford	196
38	34	49	Jason Leffler	Robinson-Blakeney Racing Toyota	77
39	31	30	David Stremme	Inception Motorsports Toyota	54
40	39	23	Scott Riggs	North Texas Pipe Chevrolet	43
41	43	37	J.J. Yeley	MaxQworkforce.com Chevrolet	32
42	38	91	Reed Sorenson	Plinker Tactical Toyota	24
43	37	87	Joe Nemechek	AM/FM Energy Wood & Pellet Stoves Toyota	22

*Sunoco Rookie of the Year Contender

NASCAR Sprint Cup Series **TOP 12** (After 25 Races)

Pos.	Driver	Points	Pos.	Driver	Points
1	GREG BIFFLE	879	7	DENNY HAMLIN	822
2	DALE EARNHARDT JR	871	8	CLINT BOWYER	811
3	MATT KENSETH	858	9	KEVIN HARVICK	807
4	JIMMIE JOHNSON	848	10	TONY STEWART	769
5	MARTIN TRUEX JR	838	11	KASEY KAHNE	751
6	BRAD KESELOWSKI	831	12	KYLE BUSCH	746

Opposite page top: Ryan Newman crawls out unhurt from his steaming Chevrolet after crashing on the backstretch with two other cars in the AdvoCare 500.

Opposite page bottom: Denny Hamlin (No. 11) leads Jeff Gordon(No. 24) and a pack of cars down the fronstretch at the 1.5-mile speedway.

Above: Teammates Tony Stewart and Ryan Newman confer in a team transporter in the garage at Atlanta Motor Speedway.

26

Richmond International Raceway
Saturday, September 8, 2012

FEDERATED AUTO PARTS 400

As capriciously as the showers came and went during the Federated Auto Parts 400 at Richmond International Raceway, so too did the hopes of Jeff Gordon and Kyle Busch in making the Chase for the NASCAR Sprint Cup.

As Clint Bowyer, already locked in the Chase, swept to his second victory of the year in his Michael Waltrip Racing No. 15 5-hour Energy Toyota, Gordon saw an almost hopeless situation magically turn around, and edged a disconsolate Busch for a Wild Card spot in the Chase playoffs.

Bowyer's trip to Victory Lane was adventurous on its own, featuring a spin on the frontstretch, which prompted his team to adopt a gas-saving strategy that worked to perfection. Well after midnight, Bowyer crossed the finish line on the 400th lap 1.198 seconds ahead of miracle-worker Gordon, who was followed by Mark Martin, Tony Stewart and Matt Kenseth.

"Thank you, Juan Pablo Montoya for wrecking me and then winning me the race," Bowyer said. The incident occurred on lap 236, and brought out one of the race's six yellow flags. "It was stupid, really," Bowyer said. "He was – I don't know how many laps down he was – I know he was at least one and we were running second or third there and he just got into us and knocked my left rear (tire) down. But, luckily I got spun out down there, got the caution and didn't go a lap down and that was the thing that won us the race. You never know. You never give up in this sport."

As Bowyer and his team calculated their way to Victory Lane, Gordon and his team went from steely resolve to despair before finally finding triumph, and this sideshow became every bit as dramatic as the main show.

Although crew chief Alan Gustafson had motivated the

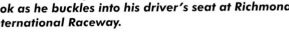

Joe Gibbs Racing driver Joey Logano sports a serious look as he buckles into his driver's seat at Richmond International Raceway.

team to a fever pitch, their Chevy's handling was a mess of looseness early in the race. You know you have problems when a pair of bolt cutters becomes the tool of choice for making chassis adjustments, as it did for Gustafson's crewmen, who had to cut a rear sway bar chain to tighten up the handling.

When the first of two rain delays brought out the red flag on lap 152, Gordon's face was a mask of tension and distress. "It's been a handful. We are working on it," he said after emerging from his car. "We just missed it. It happens."

But the bolt cutters did the trick, and Gordon's car came alive for the second half of the race. He clawed his way forward – right

into the Chase for the NASCAR Sprint Cup, capturing the Wild Card spot by three points over Busch.

"We just flat out missed the setup at the beginning," Gordon said. "Luckily, Alan and the engineers got together and found the tools that we could utilize to make the car better. The biggest thing is that rear bar – we just had to get rid of it. We did that. We cut the chain. Our car really started coming to us right then. It was amazing. I still can't believe we actually did it."

The experience was exactly the opposite for Busch and his team, who seemed to have a lock on the Wild Card spot until it all slipped away.

26 | Federated Auto Parts 400

FIN	ST	CAR	DRIVER	SPONSOR	LAPS
1	4	15	Clint Bowyer	5-hour Energy Toyota	400
2	2	24	Jeff Gordon	Drive to End Hunger Chevrolet	400
3	6	55	Mark Martin	Aaron's Dream Machine Toyota	400
4	28	14	Tony Stewart	Office Depot/Mobil 1 Chevrolet	400
5	17	17	Matt Kenseth	Best Buy Ford	400
6	20	31	Jeff Burton	Caterpillar Chevrolet	400
7	10	2	Brad Keselowski	Miller Lite Dodge	400
8	14	39	Ryan Newman	Quicken Loans Chevrolet	400
9	23	16	Greg Biffle	3M/Owens & Minor Ford	400
10	13	29	Kevin Harvick	Budweiser Chevrolet	400
11	11	22	Sam Hornish Jr	Shell Pennzoil Dodge	400
12	21	5	Kasey Kahne	Quaker State Chevrolet	399
13	5	48	Jimmie Johnson	Lowe's Chevrolet	399
14	1	88	Dale Earnhardt Jr	Diet Mountain Dew/National Guard Chevrolet	399
15	22	9	Marcos Ambrose	MAC Tools Ford	399
16	15	18	Kyle Busch	M&M's Toyota	399
17	16	99	Carl Edwards	Kellogg's Ford	399
18	7	11	Denny Hamlin	FedEx Express Toyota	399
19	12	83	Landon Cassill	Burger King Toyota	399
20	24	42	Juan Pablo Montoya	Target Chevrolet	399
21	9	56	Martin Truex Jr	NAPA Auto Parts Toyota	399
22	26	1	Jamie McMurray	Bass Pro Shops/Allstate Chevrolet	398
23	25	27	Paul Menard	Menards/Moen Chevrolet	398
24	3	78	Regan Smith	Furniture Row/Farm American Chevrolet	398
25	29	47	Bobby Labonte	Bush's Beans Toyota	397
26	18	43	Aric Almirola	Smithfield Ford	397
27	32	93	Travis Kvapil	Burger King/Dr. Pepper Toyota	397
28	30	51	Kurt Busch	Phoenix Construction Chevrolet	396
29	42	13	Casey Mears	GEICO Ford	396
30	8	20	Joey Logano	The Home Depot Toyota	396
31	35	38	David Gilliland	Mossy Oak/Pursuit Channel Ford	395
32	27	34	David Ragan	Taco Bell Ford	395
33	33	36	Dave Blaney	Tommy Baldwin Racing Chevrolet	395
34	37	10	David Reutimann	No.10 Inc. 5000-@TMone 6-peat Chevrolet	393
35	39	32	Ken Schrader	Federated Auto Parts Ford	393
36	36	33	Stephen Leicht*	Special Ops OPSEC Chevrolet	390
37	31	30	David Stremme	Inception Motorsports Chevrolet	127
38	34	87	Joe Nemechek	AM/FM Energy Wood & Pellet Stoves Toyota	90
39	38	23	Scott Riggs	North Texas Pipe Chevrolet	78
40	40	19	Mike Bliss	Plinker Tactical Toyota	70
41	19	98	Michael McDowell	Phil Parsons Racing Ford	63
42	41	26	Josh Wise*	MDS Transport Ford	57
43	43	91	Reed Sorenson	Plinker Tactical Chevrolet	57

*Sunoco Rookie of the Year Contender

NASCAR Sprint Cup Series
TOP 12
(After 26 Races)

Pos.	Driver	Points	Pos.	Driver	Points
1	DENNY HAMLIN	2,012	7	DALE EARNHARDT JR	2,003
2	JIMMIE JOHNSON	2,009	8	MATT KENSETH	2,003
3	TONY STEWART	2,009	9	KEVIN HARVICK	2,000
4	BRAD KESELOWSKI	2,009	10	MARTIN TRUEX JR	2,000
5	GREG BIFFLE	2,006	11	KASEY KAHNE	2,000
6	CLINT BOWYER	2,006	12	JEFF GORDON	2,000

Previous spread: Dale Earnhardt Jr's crew rips off a fast four-tire stop during a caution period in the Federated Auto Parts 400.

Opposite page: Clint Bowyer celebrates his second 2012 win in Victory Lane at Richmond.

Above: Furniture Row Racing driver Regan Smith, photographed while standing on pit road at Richmond, finished 24th in the race.

CHASE FOR THE NASCAR SPRINT CUP 2012

It was hard to believe that a driver as accomplished as Kyle Busch, with 24 NASCAR Sprint Cup Series victories at age 27, failed to make the 2012 Chase for the NASCAR Sprint Cup – his hopes fading on the empty sails of a single bad pit call at Richmond International Raceway after eight months of racing in 26 events. And it was equally hard to believe that a driver as great as four-time champion Jeff Gordon almost didn't make it.

But it came down to a battle among these two top contenders just to squeak into the Chase as they fought at Richmond for the final wild-card spot to be among the 12 drivers battling for the NASCAR Sprint Cup title in the season's 10 final races.

The fact that drivers of the caliber of Gordon and Busch were left to fight for the scraps was a reflection of just how intense the competition really is in the NASCAR Sprint Cup Series.

When the last of the tire smoke drifted away at Richmond, the 12 drivers in the Chase included the most recent NASCAR Sprint Cup champions as well some newcomers. Five-time champion Jimmie Johnson was in again, of course, on the strength of both his points total and his three victories. Defending champion Tony Stewart took the 10th and final spot in points, but his three wins gave him solid wild-card insurance had the points slipped away.

The top seed was Denny Hamlin, leading a strong contingent of Toyota drivers and starting the Chase in the top spot by virtue of his four victories, with 2012 points, a slim three points more than Johnson, Stewart and Brad Keselowski, all of whom had three wins.

Greg Biffle, who led the points at the end of the regular season, and had been in front after 15 of the 26 events, winning two of them, started the Chase with 2,006 points, joined by Clint Bowyer, another two-time winner.

Behind them were Dale Earnhardt Jr., and Matt Kenseth each a winner of one race, starting with 2,003 points. And bringing up the rear, starting the Chase with 2,000 points, were Kevin Harvick and Martin Truex Jr., as well as the two wild-card winners, Kasey Kahne and Gordon.

Among those besides Busch who were left to wait until 2013 to get another shot at a championship were Marcos Ambrose, Ryan Newman and Joey Logano, all of whom won a race, and the 2011 runner-up Carl Edwards.

All four of the Hendrick Motorsports Chevrolet drivers made the Chase, with Stewart and Harvick adding two more Chevrolets to the mix and putting Stewart-Haas Racing and Richard Childress Racing in the hunt. Toyota was represented by Hamlin from Joe Gibbs Racing and Michael Waltrip Racing's Bowyer and Truex, while Ford's Roush Fenway Racing had Biffle and Kenseth, with Keselowski behind the wheel of the lone Penske Racing Dodge for the 10 playoff races.

CHASE FOR THE NASCAR SPRINT CUP QUALIFYING FIELD 2012

	Poles	Wins	Top 5	Top 10
1. Denny Hamlin	2	4	11	13
2. Jimmie Johnson	1	3	12	17
3. Tony Stewart	1	3	10	12
4. Brad Keselowski	0	3	10	15
5. Greg Biffle	2	2	10	15
6. Clint Bowyer	0	2	6	15
7. Dale Earnhardt, Jr.	1	1	10	17
8. Matt Kenseth	1	1	10	16
9. Kevin Harvick	0	0	4	11
10. Martin Truex, Jr.	1	0	6	14
11. Kasey Kahne	2	2	7	13
12. Jeff Gordon	1	1	7	12

DENNY **HAMLIN**

RACE #	LOCATION	START	FINISH	POINT POS.
1	Daytona	31	4	4
2	Phoenix	13	1	1
3	Las Vegas	17	20	3
4	Bristol	20	20	5
5	Fontana	1	11	7
6	Martinsville	3	6	7
7	Texas	13	12	6
8	Kansas	4	1	5
9	Richmond	7	4	3
10	Talladega	22	23	4
11	Darlington	8	2	4
12	Charlotte	8	2	3
13	Dover	10	18	4
14	Pocono	5	5	4
15	Michigan	11	34	5
16	Sonoma	16	35	8
17	Kentucky	3	3	5
18	Daytona	23	25	7
19	Loudon	3	2	5
20	Indianapolis	1	6	5
21	Pocono	2	29	8
22	Watkins Glen	23	34	10
23	Michigan	21	11	10
24	Bristol	8	1	8
25	Atlanta	7	1	7
26	Richmond	7	18	1

JIMMIE **JOHNSON**

RACE #	LOCATION	START	FINISH	POINT POS.
1	Daytona	8	42	37
2	Phoenix	4	4	20
3	Las Vegas	6	2	13
4	Bristol	22	9	11
5	Fontana	10	10	9
6	Martinsville	22	12	10
7	Texas	10	2	8
8	Kansas	15	3	7
9	Richmond	27	6	6
10	Talladega	19	35	8
11	Darlington	2	1	5
12	Charlotte	3	11	5
13	Dover	2	1	5
14	Pocono	24	4	5
15	Michigan	10	5	4
16	Sonoma	3	5	4
17	Kentucky	1	6	3
18	Daytona	16	36	4
19	Loudon	7	7	4
20	Indianapolis	6	1	4
21	Pocono	10	14	4
22	Watkins Glen	3	3	1
23	Michigan	3	27	4
24	Bristol	37	2	2
25	Atlanta	8	34	4
26	Richmond	5	13	2

TONY **STEWART**

RACE #	LOCATION	START	FINISH	POINT POS.
1	Daytona	3	16	16
2	Phoenix	2	22	15
3	Las Vegas	7	1	7
4	Bristol	23	14	7
5	Fontana	9	1	4
6	Martinsville	15	7	3
7	Texas	29	24	7
8	Kansas	23	13	8
9	Richmond	22	3	8
10	Talladega	8	24	7
11	Darlington	17	3	7
12	Charlotte	21	25	9
13	Dover	29	25	8
14	Pocono	22	3	8
15	Michigan	8	2	8
16	Sonoma	24	2	5
17	Kentucky	22	32	9
18	Daytona	42	1	5
19	Loudon	10	12	7
20	Indianapolis	28	10	8
21	Pocono	28	5	6
22	Watkins Glen	7	19	8
23	Michigan	14	32	9
24	Bristol	21	27	10
25	Atlanta	1	22	10
26	Richmond	28	4	3

BRAD **KESELOWSK**

RACE #	LOCATION	START	FINISH	POINT POS.
1	Daytona	23	32	29
2	Phoenix	28	5	12
3	Las Vegas	20	32	22
4	Bristol	5	1	14
5	Fontana	17	18	16
6	Martinsville	7	9	12
7	Texas	8	36	15
8	Kansas	11	11	15
9	Richmond	16	9	13
10	Talladega	13	1	12
11	Darlington	15	15	12
12	Charlotte	24	5	11
13	Dover	16	12	11
14	Pocono	31	18	10
15	Michigan	25	13	10
16	Sonoma	13	12	10
17	Kentucky	8	1	10
18	Daytona	9	8	9
19	Loudon	22	5	10
20	Indianapolis	22	9	9
21	Pocono	31	4	7
22	Watkins Glen	4	2	5
23	Michigan	19	2	5
24	Bristol	2	30	7
25	Atlanta	21	3	6
26	Richmond`	10	7	4

GREG **BIFFLE**

RACE #	LOCATION	START	FINISH	POINT POS.
1	Daytona	2	3	3
2	Phoenix	7	3	2
3	Las Vegas	9	3	1
4	Bristol	1	13	1
5	Fontana	4	6	1
6	Martinsville	26	13	1
7	Texas	3	1	1
8	Kansas	17	5	1
9	Richmond	28	18	1
10	Talladega	6	5	1
11	Darlington	1	12	1
12	Charlotte	4	4	1
13	Dover	7	11	1
14	Pocono	13	24	3
15	Michigan	3	4	3
16	Sonoma	4	7	2
17	Kentucky	11	21	4
18	Daytona	4	21	3
19	Loudon	11	9	3
20	Indianapolis	5	3	3
21	Pocono	12	15	3
22	Watkins Glen	15	6	2
23	Michigan	13	1	1
24	Bristol	3	19	1
25	Atlanta	2	15	1
26	Richmond	23	9	5

CLINT **BOWYER**

RACE #	LOCATION	START	FINISH	POINT POS.
1	Daytona	30	11	11
2	Phoenix	16	30	17
3	Las Vegas	5	6	15
4	Bristol	16	4	8
5	Fontana	11	13	8
6	Martinsville	4	10	9
7	Texas	18	17	10
8	Kansas	8	36	11
9	Richmond	23	7	12
10	Talladega	24	6	10
11	Darlington	26	11	11
12	Charlotte	5	13	12
13	Dover	4	5	10
14	Pocono	16	6	9
15	Michigan	13	7	9
16	Sonoma	6	1	7
17	Kentucky	6	16	7
18	Daytona	29	29	10
19	Loudon	5	3	9
20	Indianapolis	33	15	10
21	Pocono	19	8	10
22	Watkins Glen	8	4	7
23	Michigan	12	7	7
24	Bristol	23	7	6
25	Atlanta	30	27	8
26	Richmond	4	1	6

DALE EARNHARDT, JR.

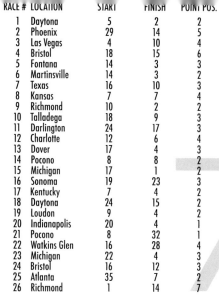

7

RACE #	LOCATION	START	FINISH	POINT POS.
1	Daytona	5	2	2
2	Phoenix	29	14	5
3	Las Vegas	4	10	4
4	Bristol	18	15	6
5	Fontana	14	3	3
6	Martinsville	14	3	2
7	Texas	16	10	3
8	Kansas	7	7	4
9	Richmond	10	2	2
10	Talladega	18	9	3
11	Darlington	24	17	3
12	Charlotte	12	6	4
13	Dover	17	4	3
14	Pocono	8	8	2
15	Michigan	17	1	2
16	Sonoma	19	23	3
17	Kentucky	7	4	2
18	Daytona	24	15	2
19	Loudon	9	4	2
20	Indianapolis	20	4	1
21	Pocono	8	32	1
22	Watkins Glen	16	28	4
23	Michigan	22	4	3
24	Bristol	16	12	3
25	Atlanta	35	7	2
26	Richmond	1	14	7

MATT KENSETH

8

RACE #	LOCATION	START	FINISH	POINT POS.
1	Daytona	4	1	1
2	Phoenix	26	13	4
3	Las Vegas	11	22	5
4	Bristol	21	2	3
5	Fontana	15	16	6
6	Martinsville	21	4	4
7	Texas	2	5	2
8	Kansas	18	4	3
9	Richmond	24	11	4
10	Talladega	10	3	2
11	Darlington	19	6	2
12	Charlotte	20	10	2
13	Dover	5	3	2
14	Pocono	14	7	1
15	Michigan	6	3	1
16	Sonoma	9	13	1
17	Kentucky	20	7	1
18	Daytona	1	3	1
19	Loudon	27	13	1
20	Indianapolis	10	35	2
21	Pocono	7	23	2
22	Watkins Glen	24	8	2
23	Michigan	4	17	2
24	Bristol	17	25	4
25	Atlanta	4	9	3
26	Richmond	17	5	8

KEVIN HARVICK

9

RACE #	LOCATION	START	FINISH	POINT POS.
1	Daytona	13	7	7
2	Phoenix	8	2	3
3	Las Vegas	3	11	2
4	Bristol	14	11	2
5	Fontana	7	4	2
6	Martinsville	2	19	5
7	Texas	15	9	5
8	Kansas	2	6	6
9	Richmond	3	19	7
10	Talladega	20	25	5
11	Darlington	23	16	8
12	Charlotte	14	8	7
13	Dover	6	2	7
14	Pocono	21	14	6
15	Michigan	2	10	6
16	Sonoma	26	16	6
17	Kentucky	4	11	6
18	Daytona	11	23	6
19	Loudon	12	8	6
20	Indianapolis	27	13	6
21	Pocono	21	16	9
22	Watkins Glen	19	15	9
23	Michigan	20	16	8
24	Bristol	13	15	9
25	Atlanta	24	5	9
26	Richmond	13	10	9

RACE #	LOCATION	START	FINISH	POINT POS.
1	Daytona	26	12	12
2	Phoenix	25	7	6
3	Las Vegas	10	17	8
4	Bristol	15	3	4
5	Fontana	13	8	5
6	Martinsville	13	5	6
7	Texas	1	6	4
8	Kansas	6	2	2
9	Richmond	8	25	5
10	Talladega	15	28	6
11	Darlington	6	5	6
12	Charlotte	15	12	6
13	Dover	18	7	6
14	Pocono	23	20	7
15	Michigan	16	12	7
16	Sonoma	5	22	9
17	Kentucky	10	8	8
18	Daytona	18	17	8
19	Loudon	4	11	8
20	Indianapolis	17	8	7
21	Pocono	15	3	5
22	Watkins Glen	9	10	6
23	Michigan	7	10	6
24	Bristol	15	11	5
25	Atlanta	28	4	5
26	Richmond	9	21	10

10

MARTIN TRUEX, JR.

RACE #	LOCATION	START	FINISH	POINT POS.
1	Daytona	20	29	26
2	Phoenix	10	34	23
3	Las Vegas	1	19	26
4	Bristol	10	37	32
5	Fontana	5	14	27
6	Martinsville	1	38	31
7	Texas	5	7	27
8	Kansas	9	8	26
9	Richmond	9	5	23
10	Talladega	5	4	19
11	Darlington	3	8	16
12	Charlotte	7	1	15
13	Dover	13	9	14
14	Pocono	10	29	16
15	Michigan	4	33	16
16	Sonoma	15	14	17
17	Kentucky	19	2	14
18	Daytona	3	7	16
19	Loudon	2	1	12
20	Indianapolis	15	12	13
21	Pocono	4	2	11
22	Watkins Glen	20	13	11
23	Michigan	5	3	11
24	Bristol	12	9	11
25	Atlanta	11	23	11
26	Richmond	21	12	11

11

KASEY KAHNE

RACE #	LOCATION	START	FINISH	POINT POS.
1	Daytona	16	40	35
2	Phoenix	30	8	23
3	Las Vegas	16	12	18
4	Bristol	4	35	23
5	Fontana	21	26	25
6	Martinsville	9	14	21
7	Texas	34	4	17
8	Kansas	20	21	18
9	Richmond	6	23	17
10	Talladega	1	33	23
11	Darlington	12	35	24
12	Charlotte	23	7	22
13	Dover	14	13	21
14	Pocono	12	19	22
15	Michigan	28	6	20
16	Sonoma	2	6	18
17	Kentucky	9	5	18
18	Daytona	5	12	17
19	Loudon	8	6	17
20	Indianapolis	9	5	15
21	Pocono	27	1	13
22	Watkins Glen	12	21	15
23	Michigan	11	28	15
24	Bristol	11	3	14
25	Atlanta	5	2	13
26	Richmond	2	2	12

12

JEFF GORDON

27

Chicagoland Speedway
Sunday, September 16, 2012

GEICO 400

It wasn't something as momentous as the passing of the torch, but just as five-time NASCAR Sprint Cup Series champion Jimmie Johnson was flaunting his strength for a possible sixth championship by dominating the GEICO 400 at Chicagoland Speedway, rising star Brad Keselowski rose up and stole the first race in the 2012 Chase for the NASCAR Sprint Cup.

Keselowski took the lead after the last round of pit stops, which were conducted under the green flag, by squeezing onto the track on the backstretch as Johnson came up from behind. Keselowski was able to hold onto the low groove and passed Johnson heading through the third turn to take the lead on lap 242 of the 267-lap event. Johnson questioned the move and NASCAR reviewed it, but called no penalty.

In any event, Keselowski checked out from there, stretching his lead during the final 26 laps in his Penske Racing No. 2 Miller Lite Dodge before speeding under the checkered flag a healthy 3.171 seconds ahead of Johnson. Kasey Kahne was third, followed by non-Chase drivers Kyle Busch and Ryan Newman.

"Is it Miller time yet?" the brash, young driver asked when there was still more than a full lap to run.

"No worries from behind," the spotter told Keselowski as he circled the 1.5-mile speedway for the final time.

It was Keselowski's fourth victory of the 2012 season and it thrust the 28-year-old Michigan driver into the Sprint Cup points lead for the first time, leaving him three points ahead of Johnson. Tony Stewart moved into third in points after finishing sixth in the race and stood eight points behind the leader. Denny Hamlin, who started the Chase in the lead, saw his race go sour on the last lap when he ran out of gas and coasted across the finish line in 16th place. He left Chicago

Drivers battle side by side by side on the 1.5-mile tri-oval at Chicagoland Speedway, with rookie Danica Patrick (No. 10) on the inside, flanked by Bobby Labonte (No. 47) and Sam Hornish Jr. (No. 22).

15 points behind Keselowski, as were Kahne and Clint Bowyer, who finished 10th.

Keselowski's car owner, Roger Penske, was elated. "Coming here to Chicago and winning the first race of the Chase is outstanding," Penske said in Victory Lane. "I can't wait to go to the next race."

Keselowski led 76 of the 267 laps, but Johnson was in front for 172 laps. "We were both showing our hand" in the final stages of the race, Keselowski said of himself and Johnson. "I don't know what happened – whether the 48 slowed down or we sped up."

Johnson had the answer for that. "The last three runs, he was definitely a factor and I was maybe a little better than him on the third-to-last, and then on the next-to-

last we were about equal, but on that last one, he was just better," Johnson said. "So congratulations to those guys, they did an awesome job, but this is a great way to start the Chase for us. It's 10 long races and a lot can happen, so to come out of here in second is a great day. . ."

The biggest loser among the Chase drivers was Jeff Gordon, who dropped out of the race and finished 35th after his throttle stuck and he slammed into the wall in turn one on lap 188. After only one event, Gordon was a whopping 47 points behind Keselowski. But with nine races to go, even Gordon still had a chance.

"This feels like round one of a heavyweight title bout," Keselowski said. "It feels good to win it. It feels great. But there's a lot of rounds left."

27 | GEICO 400

FIN	ST	CAR	DRIVER	SPONSOR	LAPS
1	13	2	Brad Keselowski	Miller Lite Dodge	267
2	1	48	Jimmie Johnson	Lowe's/Kobalt Tools Chevrolet	267
3	6	5	Kasey Kahne	Farmers Insurance Chevrolet	267
4	21	18	Kyle Busch	Wrigley Toyota	267
5	20	39	Ryan Newman	Gene Haas Foun Workshops For Warriors Chevrolet	267
6	29	14	Tony Stewart	Office Depot/Mobil 1 Chevrolet	267
7	10	20	Joey Logano	Dollar General Toyota	267
8	4	88	Dale Earnhardt Jr	AMP Energy/7-Eleven/National Guard Chevrolet	267
9	18	56	Martin Truex Jr	NAPA Auto Parts Toyota	267
10	9	15	Clint Bowyer	5-hour Energy Toyota	267
11	16	22	Sam Hornish Jr	Shell Pennzoil Dodge	267
12	35	29	Kevin Harvick	Budweiser Chevrolet	267
13	22	16	Greg Biffle	Scotch Blue Ford	267
14	15	55	Mark Martin	LG Partner of the Year/Aaron's Toyota	267
15	11	27	Paul Menard	Menards/Libman Chevrolet	267
16	8	11	Denny Hamlin	FedEx Ground Toyota	267
17	2	43	Aric Almirola	Farmland Ford	266
18	3	17	Matt Kenseth	Best Buy Ford	266
19	5	99	Carl Edwards	Fastenal Ford	266
20	14	21	Trevor Bayne	Good Sam/Camping World Ford	266
21	12	1	Jamie McMurray	McDonald's Chevrolet	266
22	37	34	David Ragan	Distraction.gov Ford	266
23	28	42	Juan Pablo Montoya	Target Chevrolet	265
24	32	31	Jeff Burton	Caterpillar Chevrolet	265
25	41	10	Danica Patrick	GoDaddy.com Chevrolet	265
26	23	47	Bobby Labonte	Bubba Burger Toyota	264
27	17	9	Marcos Ambrose	Stanley Ford	263
28	40	38	David Gilliland	1800LoanMart Ford	263
29	26	83	Landon Cassill	Burger King Toyota	262
30	39	32	T.J. Bell	U.S. Chrome Ford	261
31	38	93	Travis Kvapil	Burger King/Dr. Pepper Toyota	259
32	30	51	Kurt Busch	Phoenix Construction Chevrolet	245
33	42	36	Dave Blaney	Tommy Baldwin Racing Chevrolet	199
34	7	78	Regan Smith	Furniture Row Racing/Farm American Chevrolet	197
35	19	24	Jeff Gordon	DuPont Chevrolet	190
36	27	13	Casey Mears	GEICO Ford	146
37	36	33	Cole Whitt	LittleJoesAutos.com Chevrolet	70
38	43	26	Josh Wise*	MDS Transport Ford	66
39	31	30	David Stremme	Inception Motorsports Toyota	60
40	33	87	Joe Nemechek	AM/FM Energy Wood & Pellet Stoves Toyota	52
41	25	95	Scott Speed	JTS Ford	49
42	34	19	Mike Bliss	Plinker Tactical Toyota	41
43	24	98	Michael McDowell	Phil Parson Racing Ford	38

*Sunoco Rookie of the Year Contender

NASCAR Sprint Cup Series

TOP 12
(After 27 Races)

Pos.	Driver	Points	Pos.	Driver	Points
1	BRAD KESELOWSKI	2,056	7	DALE EARNHARDT JR	2,039
2	JIMMIE JOHNSON	2,053	8	GREG BIFFLE	2,037
3	TONY STEWART	2,048	9	MARTIN TRUEX JR	2,035
4	DENNY HAMLIN	2,041	10	KEVIN HARVICK	2,032
5	KASEY KAHNE	2,041	11	MATT KENSETH	2,030
6	CLINT BOWYER	2,041	12	JEFF GORDON	2,009

Previous spread: The 43-car field, led by pole winner Jimmie Johnson (No. 48), takes the green flag to start the GEICO 400.

Opposite page top: Martin Truex, Jr. prepares for a day of racing.

Opposite page bottom: Brad Keselowski celebrates his fourth victory of the 2012 season in Victory Lane.

Above: Jeff Gordon sports a short-lived mustache at Chicagoland Speedway before crashing out of the race and finishing 35th.

28

New Hampshire Motor Speedway
Sunday, September 23, 2012

SYLVANIA 300

Although Denny Hamlin had won more races than any-one coming to New Hampshire Motor Speedway for the second race in the Chase for the NASCAR Sprint Cup, he had also lost a few in 2012. And after a disappointing 16th-place finish at Chicagoland Speedway when he ran out of gas on the last lap, Hamlin expressed his ire and his optimism simultaneously when he tweeted: "We will win next week."

And that's exactly what Hamlin did, winning the SYLVANIA 300 in dominating fashion in his Joe Gibbs Racing No. 11 FedEx Freight Toyota after a slight stumble in qualifying forced him to start 32nd in the 43-car field. It took Hamlin 94 laps to claw through the field and get to the front in the 300-lap affair, and it was pretty much all she wrote after that, as he led 193 of the final 206 laps before crossing under the checkered flag 2.675 seconds ahead of Jimmie Johnson. Pole winner Jeff Gordon finished third, followed by Clint Bowyer and Kasey Kahne.

Hamlin capped off his victory with a grinding, seemingly endless burnout on the frontstretch of the 1.058-mile New Hampshire oval before hopping out of his car and taking a batting stance in front of the main grandstands and pointing to the heavens as he mimicked Babe Ruth and his famous "called shot" home run in the 1932 World Series.

"Yeah, you don't want to sound too cocky, but I knew what we were capable of," Hamlin said in Victory Lane. "If you're going to say something like that, you've got to run extremely well. I know we made a couple of big mistakes in the last two weeks, but I said we were fast enough to make it up and we were. This team just gave me a great car this weekend and it was just untouchable here. This is what you dream of as a race car driver to have cars like these."

Denny Hamlin was the class of the field in the SYLVANIA 300 in his Joe Gibbs Racing No. 11 FedEx Freight Toyota.

It was the 31-year-old driver's fifth victory of 2012 and his third in five weeks. But because of the stumble, he didn't take the lead in the Chase. Johnson, after finishing second in both of the first two Chase races, led the 12 drivers in the playoffs by a single point over Brad Keselowski, who won the first Chase race at Chicagoland. Keselowski finished sixth at New Hampshire. Hamlin was third in the Chase, seven points back, followed by Tony Stewart (-10), Kahne and Bowyer (-15).

"You know, when you get to the Chase, you need to execute on your great tracks and get the results you should there, and then on your tracks that aren't your best, you still have to have good days," Johnson said. "This track's been hit or miss for us over the years; so to come out of here in second, I'm real happy with today. We didn't have anything for the 11; I wish we did."

Hamlin was easily pacing the field, as he had been for the final two thirds of the race, when the race's fourth and final yellow flag flew on lap 274 for debris in turn two. That set up a final restart, with Johnson starting next to Hamlin.

But Hamlin's car was so strong, he was already checking out by the first turn. He easily dealt with this challenge – one that has doomed many a late-race leader.

Although Hamlin was happy to take full credit in calling his shot after winning the race, he spent time before the event backing off his bold prediction. He tweeted that it wasn't really a guarantee; he was just trying to pump up his Twitter followers.

"Well, when you do that (guarantee)," he said after the race, "you kind of put yourself in an island in a sense; drivers will tend to not give you the spot. They will drive harder just to make sure your job is harder. Other drivers don't like to see that happen. So you can't just call your shot and they are going to pull over and give the race to you. They are going to drive harder knowing that you've said something like that. So I just wanted it to be clear that, all right, I'm not guaranteeing anything, but barring any of those circumstances happening, we were going to win. I had faith that we were going to win."

28 | SYLVANIA 300

FIN	ST	CAR	DRIVER	SPONSOR	LAPS
1	32	11	Denny Hamlin	FedEx Freight Toyota	300
2	20	48	Jimmie Johnson	Lowe's Chevrolet	300
3	1	24	Jeff Gordon	Drive to End Hunger Chevrolet	300
4	12	15	Clint Bowyer	5-hour Energy Toyota	300
5	6	5	Kasey Kahne	Farmers Insurance Chevrolet	300
6	15	2	Brad Keselowski	Miller Lite Dodge	300
7	3	14	Tony Stewart	Mobil 1 / Office Depot Chevrolet	300
8	18	20	Joey Logano	The Home Depot Toyota	300
9	4	55	Brian Vickers	Freightliner / Jet Edge Toyota	300
10	8	39	Ryan Newman	Aspen Dental Chevrolet	300
11	16	29	Kevin Harvick	Budweiser Chevrolet	300
12	7	27	Paul Menard	Sylvania / Menards Chevrolet	300
13	14	88	Dale Earnhardt Jr	AMP Energy/Diet Mtn. Dew/Nat'l Guard Chevrolet	300
14	25	17	Matt Kenseth	Zest Ford	300
15	11	31	Jeff Burton	Wheaties Chevrolet	300
16	22	78	Regan Smith	Furniture Row / Farm American Chevrolet	300
17	9	56	Martin Truex Jr	NAPA Auto Parts Toyota	300
18	13	16	Greg Biffle	3M / GE Appliances Ford	300
19	5	99	Carl Edwards	Aflac Ford	300
20	17	47	Bobby Labonte	Bush's Beans Toyota	299
21	10	22	Sam Hornish Jr	Shell Pennzoil Dodge	299
22	24	42	Juan Pablo Montoya	Energizer Chevrolet	299
23	19	43	Aric Almirola	Trim Fit Ford	298
24	21	9	Marcos Ambrose	Stanley Ford	298
25	23	51	Kurt Busch	Phoenix Construction Chevrolet	298
26	29	1	Jamie McMurray	LiftMaster Chevrolet	298
27	28	83	Landon Cassill	Burger King / Dr Pepper Toyota	298
28	2	18	Kyle Busch	M&M's Toyota	298
29	26	34	David Ragan	Shriner's Hospital for Children Ford	297
30	34	10	David Reutimann	Tommy Baldwin Racing Chevrolet	296
31	33	93	Travis Kvapil	Burger King / Dr Pepper Toyota	296
32	37	38	David Gilliland	Taco Bell Ford	296
33	42	32	Mike Olsen	North Country Ford Ford	289
34	39	33	Stephen Leicht*	LittleJoesAutos.com Chevrolet	151
35	43	30	David Stremme	Inception Motorsports Toyota	145
36	30	13	Casey Mears	GEICO Ford	100
37	31	98	Michael McDowell	Phil Parsons Racing Ford	97
38	27	95	Scott Speed	Jordan Truck Sales Ford	88
39	36	87	Joe Nemechek	AM/FM Energy Wood Stoves/Genny Light Toyota	78
40	41	36	Tony Raines	Tommy Baldwin Racing Chevrolet	68
41	40	37	J.J. Yeley	MAXQWorkForce.com Chevrolet	29
42	35	91	Reed Sorenson	Plinker Tactical Chevrolet	21
43	38	79	Kelly Bires	BBI / Bestway Ford	20

*Sunoco Rookie of the Year Contender

NASCAR Sprint Cup Series TOP 12
(After 28 Races)

Pos.	Driver	Points	Pos.	Driver	Points
1	JIMMIE JOHNSON	2,096	7	DALE EARNHARDT JR	2,070
2	BRAD KESELOWSKI	2,095	8	KEVIN HARVICK	2,065
3	DENNY HAMLIN	2,089	9	GREG BIFFLE	2,063
4	TONY STEWART	2,086	10	MARTIN TRUEX JR	2,062
5	KASEY KAHNE	2,081	11	MATT KENSETH	2,061
6	CLINT BOWYER	2,081	12	JEFF GORDON	2,051

Previous spread: On a sunny, early fall Sunday in New Hampshire, the field rumbles through the first and second turns of the 1.058-mile oval.

Opposite page: Brian Vickers (No. 55) and Denny Hamlin (No. 11) lead Joey Logano (No. 20) and Jimmie Johnson (No. 48) in side-by-side racing at New Hampshire's low-banked speedway.

Above: Dale Earnhardt Jr. crawls out of his Chevrolet after qualifying for the SYLVANIA 300 at New Hampshire Motor Speedway.

29

Dover International Speedway
Sunday, September 30, 2012

AAA 400

Had the AAA 400 at Dover International Speedway been a matter of simple, pedal-to-the-floor horse-power, the Toyota drivers in the Joe Gibbs Racing stable would have cruised to the checkered flag as they cruised all afternoon – well in front of the rest of the field.

But all the speed meant those Toyotas of Kyle Busch and Denny Hamlin were gulping their Sunoco racing fuel. Before they could reach the finish line, the Gibbs Toyota tanks went low, and the trophy instead went to a fuel saver, Brad Keselowski, who took command of the Chase for the NASCAR Sprint Cup with his fifth victory of the year and his second in the Chase.

Skillfully saving fuel during the final 79 laps, all of which were run under the green flag, Keselowski saw the rabbits fall by the wayside as both Busch and Hamlin had to pit for fuel, while Dover's own monster dominator, Jimmie Johnson, was also crippled by a lack of gas, giving up spots in order to make it to the end, limping home in fourth place.

At the end of lap 400, Keselowski streaked under the flag in his Penske Racing No. 2 Miller Lite Dodge 1.078 seconds ahead of Jeff Gordon. Mark Martin was third, followed by Johnson and Carl Edwards. The only other driver to finish on the lead lap was Martin Truex, Jr. in sixth, followed by Busch and Hamlin, both a lap down after their late pit stops. Busch had dominated, leading 302 laps, while Hamlin had been in front for 39 laps.

"As the race went on, we slowly eked our way up from the 10th starting position we had up to fourth," Keselowski said in the winner's interview. "Kind of fell in there on that last run, after my pit crew got me out fourth, something like that, and that put us in position to really capitalize on good strategy and execution. My guys did that. They did a great job, like you

The fast Joe Gibbs Racing Toyotas driven by pole winner Denny Hamlin (No. 11) and Kyle Busch (No. 18) pace the field before a restart at Dover International Speedway.

said, with the fuel. Together we were able to manage it very well, which is important as anything else in racing these days. As you saw, it came together at the end for a victory."

Keselowski was not supposed to win here, or even run that well, having averaged only a 17th place finish in five previous starts. This was Johnson's stadium, with seven victories on the one-mile high-banked oval, several of which helped propel him to NASCAR Sprint Cup championships.

"This hasn't been one of our best tracks, but we talked on the plane ride up here and felt that we were capable of winning here this weekend," Keselowski's crew chief, Paul Wolfe, said. "I think that type of mentality and attitude is throughout our team. I feel like there was a lot of hard work that went in behind the scenes preparing for this weekend. We were able to unload here and have good speed in our car. I feel much better than what we've

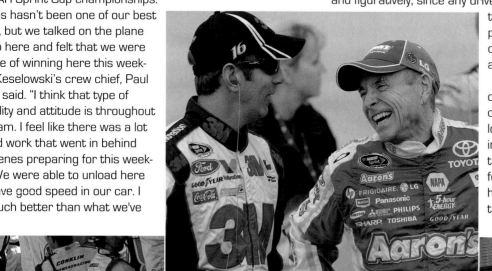

been in the past. I think we backed that up with a solid qualifying effort (10th) yesterday afternoon (and) just slowly worked on our car all day. It took us probably two runs to get it capable of running in the top five."

Keselowski opened the Chase with a victory in Chicago, and with his second win in three races, he moved to the front of the Chase field both literally, holding a five-point lead over Johnson, and figuratively, since any driver who can win a Chase race at a track where he hasn't run well in the past would seem to possess enough of that special Chase magic to win it all.

"It feels great to win. I'm so proud of my team," Keselowski said. "But I can't state loudly enough how much longer this battle is. It's very tempting, whether it's the media or the teams themselves, to get in a comfort zone of saying, 'Such and such has control of this Chase.' But there's a reason why it's 10 rounds.

29 | AAA 400

FIN	ST	CAR	DRIVER	SPONSOR	LAPS
1	10	2	Brad Keselowski	Miller Lite Dodge	400
2	7	24	Jeff Gordon	Drive to End Hunger Chevrolet	400
3	26	55	Mark Martin	Aaron's 2000th Store - Bronx, NY Toyota	400
4	11	48	Jimmie Johnson	Lowe's/Kobalt Tools Chevrolet	400
5	15	99	Carl Edwards	Fastenal Ford	400
6	3	56	Martin Truex Jr	NAPA Auto Parts Toyota	400
7	5	18	Kyle Busch	Interstate Batteries Toyota	399
8	1	11	Denny Hamlin	FedEx Office Toyota	399
9	2	15	Clint Bowyer	5-hour Energy Toyota	399
10	14	20	Joey Logano	The Home Depot Toyota	399
11	25	88	Dale Earnhardt Jr	National Guard/Diet Mountain Dew Chevrolet	398
12	17	6	Ricky Stenhouse Jr	Cargill Ford	397
13	13	29	Kevin Harvick	Budweiser Chevrolet	397
14	16	47	Bobby Labonte	Kingsford Charcoal Toyota	397
15	9	5	Kasey Kahne	Farmers Insurance Chevrolet	397
16	6	16	Greg Biffle	Scotch-Brite Ford	397
17	18	78	Regan Smith	Furniture Row/Farm American Chevrolet	397
18	27	9	Marcos Ambrose	DeWalt Ford	397
19	21	43	Aric Almirola	Super 8 Ford	397
20	24	14	Tony Stewart	Office Depot/Mobil 1 Chevrolet	397
21	8	39	Ryan Newman	U.S. ARMY Chevrolet	397
22	19	27	Paul Menard	Menards/CertainTeed Chevrolet	396
23	28	51	Kurt Busch	Phoenix Construction Chevrolet	395
24	20	1	Jamie McMurray	McDonald's Chevrolet	394
25	4	22	Sam Hornish Jr	Shell Pennzoil Dodge	393
26	35	42	Juan Pablo Montoya	Target Chevrolet	393
27	39	31	Jeff Burton	Caterpillar Chevrolet	393
28	38	10	Danica Patrick	GoDaddy.com Chevrolet	393
29	33	93	Travis Kvapil	Burger King Toyota	392
30	31	34	David Ragan	Long John Silver's Ford	392
31	30	13	Casey Mears	GEICO Ford	391
32	42	38	David Gilliland	Taco Bell Ford	391
33	41	32	T.J. Bell	Green Smoke Ford	390
34	40	36	J.J. Yeley	Drive Sober, Arrive Alive DE Chevrolet	388
35	12	17	Matt Kenseth	Ford EcoBoost Ford	371
36	22	83	Landon Cassill	Burger King Toyota	354
37	23	26	Josh Wise*	MDS Transport Ford	92
38	32	98	Michael McDowell	Phil Parsons Racing Ford	51
39	37	87	Joe Nemechek	AM/FM Energy Wood & Pellet Stoves Toyota	48
40	34	95	Scott Speed	Jordan Truck Sales Ford	32
41	43	37	Dave Blaney	MaxQWorkforce.com Chevrolet	29
42	36	23	Scott Riggs	North Texas Pipe Chevrolet	26
43	29	91	Reed Sorenson	Plinker Tactical Toyota	18

*Sunoco Rookie of the Year Contender

NASCAR Sprint Cup Series

TOP 12
(After 29 Races)

Pos.	Driver	Points	Pos.	Driver	Points
1	BRAD KESELOWSKI	2,142	7	DALE EARNHARDT JR	2,103
2	JIMMIE JOHNSON	2,137	8	MARTIN TRUEX JR	2,100
3	DENNY HAMLIN	2,126	9	KEVIN HARVICK	2,096
4	CLINT BOWYER	2,117	10	JEFF GORDON	2,094
5	TONY STEWART	2,110	11	GREG BIFFLE	2,091
6	KASEY KAHNE	2,110	12	MATT KENSETH	2,070

Previous spread: Race winner Brad Keselowski (No. 2) burns the rubber off his Goodyear Eagle racing tires during a patriotically monumental burnout after the AAA 400.

Opposite page top: Greg Biffle and Mark Martin share a laugh during a quieter moment at the track.

Opposite page bottom: Denny Hamlin's pit crew changes the right side tires before doing the other side, all in a matter of seconds.

Above: Kasey Kahne pauses for a moment on pit road at Dover International Raceway.

30

Talladega Superspeedway
Sunday, October 7, 2012

GOOD SAM ROADSIDE ASSISTANCE 500

Never has the phrase "win or go bust" seemed more appropriate for a race than for the Good Sam Roadside Assistance 500 at Talladega Superspeedway, which saw an action-packed but largely trouble-free race punctuated by an insane final lap in which just about every driver except winner Matt Kenseth wrecked in a fourth-turn accident.

Almost lonely looking in the absence of other cars, Kenseth crossed the finish line in his Roush Fenway Racing No. 17 EcoBoost/National Breast Cancer Foundation Ford as the yellow flag flew, with Gordon trailing some distance back and Kyle Busch trailing him.

Although Busch only slammed into Gordon's rear bumper during the crash and didn't lose control, he was listed as having been involved, as were David Ragan and Regan Smith, who finished fourth and fifth. Four of the other five drivers who finished in the top 10 also were caught up in the 25-car accident.

Kenseth's win, his first at Talladega, underscored his team's strength in the restrictor-plate races, having also won the Daytona 500. And it provided a boost for a driver and team who had started the Chase with three straight poor finishes, the best being a 14th-place finish at New Hampshire.

"It feels great this year," Kenseth said in Victory Lane. "I'm not sure it balances out. I feel like I'm pretty clumsy at plate racing my whole career and never had a lot of great finishes, but I'm glad the plan came together."

The stage was set for the dramatic, metal-crunching last lap by a moment of chaos that was but a hint of things to come. With just over five laps to go in the scheduled race, Jamie McMurray couldn't hang onto his squirrelly car in the shove-and-bump pack and went sailing out of control down

The racing is four-wide at Talladega as Marcos Ambrose (No. 9) battles on the inside of eventual race winner Matt Kenseth (No. 17), who is below Dale Earnhardt Jr. (No. 88) and Aric Almirola (No. 43).

into the tri-oval grass. When his car came back up on the track, backmarkers had to dodge him. But no one hit him and he hit nothing except the grass, which tore up his front end and took him out of the race after a strong effort that saw him lead 38 laps.

Thus it came down to a green-white-checkered overtime finish, with an extra lap tacked onto the 188-lap event. Kenseth led at the restart, but as the tightly packed field started the last lap, Tony Stewart shot out in front. And through most of the final circuit, Stewart was in front, with Kenseth right behind, and the swarming field behind them.

As they all roared through the fourth turn, veteran Michael Waltrip, now only an occasional competitor, saw racing glory over the top of his steering wheel as he drafted at the front of a long line of cars that was fast pushing him to the front. Stewart saw the threat too late. He tried to block, but was hooked by Waltrip instead. His Chevy flipped, twirled and tumbled above and into the field behind him.

"I just screwed up," Stewart said afterwards. "I turned down

across, I think it was Michael, and crashed the whole field. It was my fault blocking to try to stay where I was at. So, I take 100% of the blame."

Brad Keselowski, leader in the Chase for the NASCAR Sprint Cup, managed to finished seventh despite being involved in the crash, which boosted his lead in the Chase by nine points, giving him a 14-point edge over Johnson, who finished 17th. Denny Hamlin was third in the points, 23 back, followed by Kasey Kahne (-36) and Clint Bowyer (-40).

Despite his victory, Kenseth remained 12th in the 12-driver Chase, 62 points behind Keselowski and 11 points behind of Dale Earnhardt Jr. in 11th. Four days after the race, however, Earnhardt effectively ended his championship hopes when he announced that symptoms of a concussion he received in a crash in testing in August had reappeared after the crash at Talladega, forcing him to skip the next two events, the races at Charlotte and Kansas. Regan Smith was named to replace the sport's most popular driver for those two events.

30 | Good Sam Roadside Assistance 500

FIN	ST	CAR	DRIVER	SPONSOR	LAPS
1	15	17	Matt Kenseth	Ford EcoBoost/Nat'l Breast Cancer Foun Ford	189
2	6	24	Jeff Gordon	Drive to End Hunger Chevrolet	189
3	13	18	Kyle Busch	M&M's Toyota	189
4	25	34	David Ragan	MHP-8 hour Alert Ford	189
5	28	78	Regan Smith	Furniture Row / Farm American Chevrolet	189
6	5	16	Greg Biffle	3M / National Breast Cancer Foundation Ford	189
7	22	2	Brad Keselowski	Miller Lite Dodge	189
8	36	93	Travis Kvapil	Burger King / Dr Pepper Toyota	189
9	2	39	Ryan Newman	U.S. Army Chevrolet	189
10	26	31	Jeff Burton	Caterpillar / DriveCat.com Chevrolet	189
11	21	29	Kevin Harvick	Budweiser Chevrolet	189
12	1	5	Kasey Kahne	Hendrickcars.com Chevrolet	189
13	9	56	Martin Truex Jr	NAPA Auto Parts Toyota	189
14	23	11	Denny Hamlin	FedEx Freight Toyota	189
15	32	38	David Gilliland	Peanut Patch Boiled Peanuts/M. Holmes Ford	189
16	31	32	Terry Labonte	C&J Energy Services Ford	189
17	17	48	Jimmie Johnson	Lowe's Chevrolet	189
18	40	47	Bobby Labonte	Scott / Kingsford / Bush Beans Toyota	189
19	18	43	Aric Almirola	Gwaltney Ford	189
20	12	88	Dale Earnhardt Jr	Diet Mountain Dew Paint 88/Nat'l Guard Chev	189
21	8	21	Trevor Bayne	Motorcraft / Quick Lane / Warriors in Pink Ford	189
22	4	14	Tony Stewart	Mobil 1 / Office Depot Chevrolet	188
23	3	15	Clint Bowyer	5-hour Energy/Avon Foun for Women Toyota	188
24	10	22	Sam Hornish Jr	SKF Dodge	188
25	11	55	Michael Waltrip	Charlie Loudermilk Aaron's Dream Machine Toyota	188
26	19	13	Casey Mears	GEICO Ford	188
27	20	9	Marcos Ambrose	DeWalt Ford	188
28	16	27	Paul Menard	Certain Teed Insulation / Menards Chevrolet	188
29	39	36	Dave Blaney	Golden Corral Chevrolet	188
30	38	83	Landon Cassill	Burger King / Dr Pepper Toyota	188
31	34	98	Michael McDowell	K-LOVE / Curb Records Ford	188
32	14	20	Joey Logano	The Home Depot Toyota	187
33	30	30	David Stremme	SwanEnergyInc.com Toyota	187
34	24	1	Jamie McMurray	Bass Pro Shops / Allstate Chevrolet	184
35	43	23	Robert Richardson	North Texas Pipe Toyota	180
36	7	99	Carl Edwards	Subway Ford	179
37	41	10	David Reutimann	CVP@Tmone.com Chevrolet	162
38	27	42	Juan Pablo Montoya	Target / Gillette Chevrolet	156
39	29	51	Kurt Busch	Phoenix Construction Chevrolet	98
40	42	33	Cole Whitt	LittleJoesAutos.com Chevrolet	16
41	37	87	Joe Nemechek	AM/FM Energy Wood & Pellet Stoves Toyota	12
42	35	97	Timmy Hill	AM/FM Energy Wood Stoves/SWM Toyota	8
43	33	26	Josh Wise*	MDS Transport Ford	5

*Sunoco Rookie of the Year Contender

NASCAR Sprint Cup Series TOP 12
(After 30 Races)

Pos.	Driver	Points	Pos.	Driver	Points
1	BRAD KESELOWSKI	2,179	7	TONY STEWART	2,133
2	JIMMIE JOHNSON	2,165	8	MARTIN TRUEX JR	2,131
3	DENNY HAMLIN	2,156	9	GREG BIFFLE	2,130
4	KASEY KAHNE	2,143	10	KEVIN HARVICK	2,130
5	CLINT BOWYER	2,139	11	DALE EARNHARDT JR	2,128
6	JEFF GORDON	2,137	12	MATT KENSETH	2,117

Previous spread: For much of the field, the Good Sam Roadside Assistance 500 ended in a metal-crunching smashup in turn four of the last lap that involved 25 cars.

Opposite page: With five laps to go, Jamie McMurray (No. 1) lost control in the tri-oval, which brought out a yellow flag and set the stage for the final green-white-checkered overtime finish.

Above: Jimmie Johnson's daughter, Genevieve, stands on tiptoes to check out her dad's car on pit road at Talladega Superspeedway.

31

Charlotte Motor Speedway
Saturday, October 13, 2012

BANK OF AMERICA 500

Clint Bowyer's crew chief, Brian Pattie, knew that their Michael Waltrip Racing No. 15 5-hour Energy/Avon Foundation for Women Toyota was not as fast as other cars in the Bank of America 500 field at Charlotte Motor Speedway. And when you can't outrun 'em, you'd better have other options, Pattie would tell folks after engineering a perfect fuel-mileage strategy that allowed Bowyer to win his third race of the year.

Bowyer ran the 500 miles with one pit stop less than most of the rest of the field and cruised under the checkered flag 0.417 of a second ahead of Denny Hamlin. Jimmie Johnson was third, followed by Greg Biffle and Kyle Busch as all of the top finishers were forced to conserve fuel in a race that saw only five yellow flags and none at all during the final 107 laps of the 334-lap event.

"I can't do a burnout," Bowyer said in Victory Lane. "The thing doesn't have enough fuel in it to do a burnout. I'd like to practice a burnout. It's so much fun burning rubber. Hell, I don't care. I'll tell you, it's a lot more fun handing that trophy over he's fixing to hand me – that's what it's all about."

Bowyer walked to Victory Lane, and when he kidded his crew chief about showing up late with the car, Pattie quipped, "This is the third time that we've won and the third time we had to push it to Victory Lane. It would be nice to win one of these things and actually drive to Victory Lane."

Brad Keselowski, leading the points in the Chase for the NASCAR Sprint Cup, was the leader during much of this race, too, pacing the field for 139 laps. But crew chiefs up and down pit road could see the handwriting on the wall, and realized that if the race remained under the green flag, a fuel-saving strategy over the course of the last two runs would make the difference between winning and losing.

A tire specialist on Tony Stewart's team uses a portable lantern to help make sure he's precise as he glues lugnuts to one of Stewart's left-side wheels.

This included Keselowski, but he tried to stretch it too far and ran out of gas while leading on 275. He eventually finished 11th, one lap down.

"It's like playing blackjack," Keselowski said. "Sometimes you get a good deal, but you're not going to win them all. You know that, and you hope that when you're sitting there with 13 that you can just not have a lot of chips in the pile. We didn't lose too much. We got 11th out of a day where everything kind of fell against us."

In the final 75 laps, as other drivers began peeling off to the pits for gas, Bowyer backed off the power and stretched the gas. He finally pitted on lap 278 – three laps after Keselowski ran out – and then managed to run the final 55 laps without stopping again. Hamlin and Johnson used similar strategies, and

though they both had the power to pass Bowyer, they couldn't risk using it lest they gulp up all of their Sunoco fuel before the end.

Keselowski still led the Chase at the end of the race, but his lead had shrunk to seven points over Johnson, who continued to rack up good finishes. Hamlin was third, 15 points behind, while Bowyer moved into the picture, 28 points behind after his first Chase victory.

"To be back in Victory Lane, new life, new hope going into Kansas, there's a lot of races left," said Bowyer. "You know, I looked at it last week and going into this week, and I still thought if one of those guys were to stub a toe – if Brad stubbed his toe – it really opened the door for about eight of us right back into the championship hunt. With a win here, it definitely gave us new life and new hope."

31 | Bank of America 500

FIN	ST	CAR	DRIVER	SPONSOR	LAPS
1	4	15	Clint Bowyer	5-hour Energy/Avon Foun for Women Toyota	334
2	9	11	Denny Hamlin	FedEx Ground Toyota	334
3	5	48	Jimmie Johnson	Mylowes Chevrolet	334
4	1	16	Greg Biffle	3M/IDG Ford	334
5	8	18	Kyle Busch	M&M's Toyota	334
6	2	55	Mark Martin	Aaron's Dream Machine Toyota	334
7	19	99	Carl Edwards	Kellogg's Ford	333
8	10	5	Kasey Kahne	Time Warner Cable Chevrolet	333
9	12	20	Joey Logano	The Home Depot Toyota	333
10	6	56	Martin Truex Jr	NAPA Auto Parts Toyota	333
11	20	2	Brad Keselowski	Miller Lite Dodge	333
12	17	43	Aric Almirola	Smithfield Ford	333
13	32	14	Tony Stewart	Mobil 1/Office Depot Chevrolet	333
14	7	17	Matt Kenseth	Best Buy Ford	333
15	14	22	Sam Hornish Jr	Shell Pennzoil Dodge	333
16	11	29	Kevin Harvick	Jimmy John's Chevrolet	333
17	30	1	Jamie McMurray	McDonald's Chevrolet	333
18	13	24	Jeff Gordon	Drive to End Hunger Chevrolet	332
19	22	42	Juan Pablo Montoya	Target/Kellogg's Chevrolet	332
20	3	39	Ryan Newman	Quicken Loans Chevrolet	332
21	21	78	Kurt Busch	Furniture Row/Farm American Chevrolet	332
22	16	21	Trevor Bayne	Good Sam/Camping World Ford	332
23	36	38	David Gilliland	Glory Foods Ford	331
24	38	51	AJ Allmendinger	Phoenix Construction Chevrolet	330
25	41	93	Travis Kvapil	Dr Pepper Toyota	330
26	37	83	Landon Cassill	Burger King Toyota	329
27	24	27	Paul Menard	Menards/Pittsburgh Paints Chevrolet	328
28	39	31	Jeff Burton	Caterpillar Chevrolet	327
29	27	13	Casey Mears	GEICO Ford	327
30	34	10	David Reutimann	TBR/TMone.com Chevrolet	327
31	33	98	Michael McDowell	K-Love/Curb Records Ford	326
32	15	47	Bobby Labonte	Scott Brand Toyota	324
33	18	9	Marcos Ambrose	Stanley Ford	303
34	25	34	David Ragan	Glory Foods Ford	287
35	29	6	Ricky Stenhouse Jr	Best Buy Ford	190
36	40	32	Timmy Hill	U.S. Chrome Ford	182
37	31	30	David Stremme	Inception Motorsports Toyota	62
38	26	88	Regan Smith	AMP Energy/National Guard Chevrolet	61
39	28	19	Mike Bliss	Plinker Tactical Toyota	53
40	23	95	Scott Speed	B&D Electrical Ford	50
41	43	91	Reed Sorenson	Aquaria USA Toyota	32
42	35	37	J.J. Yeley	MaxQWorkForce.com Chevrolet	30
43	42	36	Dave Blaney	Tommy Baldwin Racing Chevrolet	25

*Sunoco Rookie of the Year Contender

NASCAR Sprint Cup Series TOP 12
(After 31 Races)

Pos.	Driver	Points	Pos.	Driver	Points
1	BRAD KESELOWSKI	2,214	7	MARTIN TRUEX JR	2,165
2	JIMMIE JOHNSON	2,207	8	TONY STEWART	2,164
3	DENNY HAMLIN	2,199	9	JEFF GORDON	2,164
4	CLINT BOWYER	2,186	10	KEVIN HARVICK	2,158
5	KASEY KAHNE	2,179	11	MATT KENSETH	2,147
6	GREG BIFFLE	2,171	12	DALE EARNHARDT JR	2,128

Previous spread: The grand spectacle that is NASCAR Sprint Cup Series racing unfolds at Charlotte Motor Speedway as eventual race winner Clint Bowyer leads the field toward turn one.

Opposite page top: Before the race, tightrope artist Nik Wallenda thrilled the crowd with a 750-foot stroll on a high wire strung 100 feet above the speedway infield.

Opposite page bottom: Matt Kenseth (No. 17) took this spin in turn four on lap 11 on his way to a 14th-place finish, one lap down.

Above: Clint Bowyer, the gas-saving master of the 2012 season, had to wait yet again in Victory Lane until his fuel-starved car could be pushed there.

32

Kansas Speedway
Sunday, October 21, 2012

HOLLYWOOD CASINO 400

The Hollywood Casino 400 was one of the wildest races of the year, but the mayhem was evenly distributed among the frontrunners in the Chase for the NASCAR Sprint Cup, so little movement happened in the tight championship points race as Matt Kenseth out-survived the field to win his second race in three events.

Kenseth smacked the wall himself midway through the race, but in this crazy event, the bad luck turned into good luck, putting him out of sequence with the rest of the field on pit stops, which served to help allow him to run in front at the end of the race. Kenseth led 78 of the 267 laps, including the final 49 laps, before crossing the finish line in his Roush Fenway Racing No. 17 Zest Ford 0.495 of a second ahead of Martin Truex Jr. Paul Menard was third, followed by Kasey Kahne and Tony Stewart.

"Our race went pretty good," Kenseth said after scoring his third victory of the season in a race slowed by 14 yellow flags, more than any other race of the season. "Our car wasn't bad from the start. Pretty good until I got into the wall. We had to come and fix it. Actually turned out to be some good fortune. Didn't slow the car down. Had more fuel than anybody. They had to wait to fill their tanks up and we got our tank full faster, plus we had a really good pit stop, were able to pass all those guys. Put me out front and gave us a chance."

The veteran driver, enjoying a fruitful 14th and final campaign with Roush Fenway Racing was emotional in victory lane. "You never know when or if your next win is," Kenseth said in the winner's interview. "Like I always am, especially as you get older, you really appreciate it more. I'm really, really thankful and humble to be sitting up here, honestly."

Brad Keselowski, who came into the race leading the

After streaking to his third victory of the year, Matt Kenseth holds his daughter, Grace, as he celebrates in Victory Lane with his wife, Katie, and other daughter, Kaylin.

Chase for the NASCAR Sprint Cup by seven points over Jimmie Johnson, departed with precisely the same lead, but perhaps with a few gray hairs on his young head after salvaging an eighth-place finish.

"I don't even know how to explain it," he said afterwards. "I'm ready to go home and have a couple of beers. It's just been a long day and, you know, everybody has been asking all season long where the cautions have been. Well, they flew to Kansas and they've been hanging out here because there was caution after caution and it seemed like every wreck that happened today happened right in front of me. So I'm glad to have survived the carnage and brought back a decent car, my Miller Lite Dodge, in great shape and dodged a bullet of a race. Whew! Just a tough day."

The day was even tougher for Johnson, which made his ninth-place finish all the more remarkable. Johnson had been shuffled back in the field when he pitted under the green flag while leading, only to see a yellow flag fly.

Driving among the backmarkers, Johnson lost control and backed into the wall on lap 136, doing significant damage to the back of his car.

With a skillful pit crew, and almost half the race left to recover, Johnson and his team did just that, repeatedly making additional repairs during pit stops under the generous allotment of late-race yellow flags. Somehow, he made it back into the top 10, one spot behind Keselowski. And the fact that he led laps and Keselowski didn't meant they finished with the same number of points.

"I'm definitely proud of this team, and the fact that we never give up," Johnson said. "We continue to fight to try to get every point that we can. All that said, I'm very proud, but also disappointed. I crashed the car. I spun out trying to get inside the No. 56 (driven by Truex). He bobbled a little in front of me and I thought that was an opportunity to jump in the gas real hard. When I did that, my car took off and I couldn't catch it."

Denny Hamlin remained third in the Chase, but lost five points, falling to 20 points back, after struggling to a 13th-place finish. "I drove to the top five on the first run and then we took four (tires) and the entire field took two, and that put us in the back of the pack and we were no better than the backmarkers at that point," Hamlin said.

Clint Bowyer moved up the ladder a bit while holding onto fourth place, gaining three points with a sixth-place finish. He's now 25 points behind Keselowski. Kahne remained in fifth, now 30 points behind. And despite winning two of three races, Kenseth was still way back in the standings, sitting in ninth place, 55 points behind Keselowski, with only four races left to go.

32 | Hollywood Casino 400

FIN	ST	CAR	DRIVER	SPONSOR	LAPS
1	12	17	Matt Kenseth	Zest Ford	267
2	16	56	Martin Truex Jr	NAPA Auto Parts Toyota	267
3	14	27	Paul Menard	Menards/CertainTeed Insulation Chevrolet	267
4	1	5	Kasey Kahne	Farmers Insurance Chevrolet	267
5	33	14	Tony Stewart	Office Depot/Mobil 1 Chevrolet	267
6	3	15	Clint Bowyer	5-hour Energy/Avon Foun. for Women Toyota	267
7	39	88	Regan Smith	National Guard/Diet Mountain Dew Chevrolet	267
8	25	2	Brad Keselowski	Miller Lite Dodge	267
9	7	48	Jimmie Johnson	Lowe's Chevrolet	267
10	19	24	Jeff Gordon	DuPont Chevrolet	267
11	10	29	Kevin Harvick	Budweiser Chevrolet	267
12	18	9	Marcos Ambrose	Black & Decker Ford	267
13	9	11	Denny Hamlin	FedEx Freight Toyota	267
14	17	99	Carl Edwards	Fastenal Ford	267
15	21	1	Jamie McMurray	Bass Pro Shops/Arctic Cat Chevrolet	267
16	24	42	Juan Pablo Montoya	Taylor Swift/Target Chevrolet	267
17	31	93	Travis Kvapil	Burger King/Dr Pepper Toyota	267
18	26	83	Landon Cassill	Burger King Toyota	267
19	8	20	Joey Logano	Dollar General Toyota	267
20	37	34	David Ragan	Client One Securities LLC Ford	267
21	32	21	Trevor Bayne	Motorcraft/Quick Lane Tire & Auto Center Ford	267
22	42	32	Timmy Hill	Southern Pride Trucking/U.S. Chrome Ford	267
23	38	38	David Gilliland	Long John Silver's Ford	266
24	2	55	Mark Martin	Aaron's Dream Machine Toyota	266
25	29	78	Kurt Busch	Furniture Row/Farm American Chevrolet	265
26	15	22	Sam Hornish Jr	Shell Pennzoil Dodge	234
27	11	16	Greg Biffle	3M/Sherwin-Williams Ford	227
28	20	31	Jeff Burton	Caterpillar Chevrolet	214
29	5	43	Aric Almirola	Farmland Ford	212
30	6	39	Ryan Newman	Code 3 Associates Chevrolet	188
31	4	18	Kyle Busch	M&M's Halloween Toyota	181
32	40	10	Danica Patrick	GoDaddy Racing Chevrolet	154
33	22	47	Bobby Labonte	Kingsford Charcoal Toyota	140
34	35	95	Scott Speed	B&D Electrical Ford	77
35	13	51	AJ Allmendinger	Phoenix Construction Chevrolet	69
36	30	19	Mike Bliss	Plinker Tactical/Crowne Plaza Toyota	47
37	28	13	Casey Mears	GEICO Ford	29
38	43	79	Kelly Bires	Bestway Disposal/Re-Load.biz Ford	28
39	41	36	Dave Blaney	TBR/TMone Chevrolet	25
40	36	87	Joe Nemechek	AM/FM Energy Wood & Pellet Stoves Toyota	22
41	34	91	Reed Sorenson	Plinker Tactical/Crowne Plaza Toyota	18
42	27	37	J.J. Yeley	MaxQWorkForce.com Chevrolet	11
43	23	98	Michael McDowell	K-Love/Curb Records Ford	7

*Sunoco Rookie of the Year Contender

NASCAR Sprint
Cup Series

TOP 12
(After 32 Races)

Pos.	Driver	Points	Pos.	Driver	Points
1	BRAD KESELOWSKI	2,250	7	TONY STEWART	2,203
2	JIMMIE JOHNSON	2,243	8	JEFF GORDON	2,199
3	DENNY HAMLIN	2,230	9	MATT KENSETH	2,195
4	CLINT BOWYER	2,225	10	KEVIN HARVICK	2,191
5	KASEY KAHNE	2,220	11	GREG BIFFLE	2,188
6	MARTIN TRUEX JR	2,207	12	DALE EARNHARDT JR	2,128

Previous spread: Matt Kenseth (No. 17) leads a pack of snarling NASCAR Sprint Cup Series cars across the start-finish line on a restart in the Hollywood Casino 400.

Opposite page: Jimmie Johnson smashed up the back end of his Chevrolet on lap 136, but the gas man still had a place to put the gas, so Johnson was able to recover and finish ninth.

Above: A young NASCAR fan cranes his neck to try to see inside Ryan Newman's Stewart-Haas Racing No. 39 Code 3 Associates Chevrolet.

33

Martinsville Speedway
Sunday, October 28, 2012

TUMS FAST RELIEF 500

Coming into the TUMS Fast Relief 500 at Martinsville Speedway, Jimmie Johnson had been consistent if not all that flashy in his campaign to win a sixth NASCAR Sprint Cup Series championship in seven years.

But at Martinsville, one of Johnson's favorite playgrounds, the five-time champ stopped flying under the radar and took command of the Chase for the NASCAR Sprint Cup with a dominating victory in the 500-lap slugfest on NASCAR's smallest track.

Johnson led 193 laps, including the final 15 circuits on the .526-mile short track before taking the checkered flag with a healthy 0.479 of a second lead over Kyle Busch. Kasey Kahne was third, followed by Aric Almirola and Clint Bowyer.

The victory, Johnson's fourth of the year but his first in the Chase, propelled him into the championship lead with a miniscule two-point edge over Brad Keselowski, who skillfully hung in there, battling to a sixth-place finish.

"I'm ecstatic about the win today and ecstatic about the point lead, but this is no cakewalk," Johnson said in Victory Lane. "These guys are bringing their best each and every week and we've got to keep working hard to keep this Lowe's Chevy up front; and we're in good shape."

Johnson's confidence underscored the fact that a two-point lead is not meaningless when held by a driver of his caliber. With only three races left, Keselowski faced the daunting challenge of outperforming a world-class champion who has twice as much experience as anyone else when it comes to winning the Chase. In the unlikely event that both of the leaders stumble, Bowyer (26 points behind) and Kahne (29 points back) could be right back in it.

Keselowski's sixth-place finish was his best in six starts at the southern Virginia short track and "means you can't count

Jimmie Johnson (No. 48) leads the field under the green flag and toward the tight first turn during a late-race restart in the TUMS Fast Relief 500 at Martinsville Speedway.

this team out," he said afterwards. "This championship is going to come down to Homestead. You have to be in a position where you're within shot of it. We have to do what we need to do to be in contention at Homestead."

The big victim of the day was Denny Hamlin, who had come to Martinsville only 20 points from the lead. But he had nothing but trouble at one of his best tracks. He incurred two speeding penalties on pit road and fought back through the pack after both of them, only to fall victim to a rare mechanical failure.

"Just to have to go through a day like that and it end like this is tough, especially on our best race track," Hamlin said. "Going through the adversity of speeding twice and still driving back to the front – it's frustrating. What can you do? We broke a bolt on a master switch and it ended our Chase chances." Hamlin fell to fifth place in the Chase, 49 points behind Johnson.

The victory was Johnson's seventh at Martinsville and the 59th career win for a driver still in his prime. "I think in order to be the champion, the tracks you know you can win at you have to win at," Johnson said in the winner's interview. "We did that today. We've done a very nice job over these seven races to put ourselves in the points lead. We've had a variety of different races finish with fuel mileage and things like that that have kept us out of Victory Lane and certainly played into their hands. We're ready to race under any conditions. Next two races will tell the tale. Anything can happen. We could both wad it up next week and Clint Bowyer is your champion. You never know. You got to go race the race."

33 | TUMS Fast Relief 500

FIN	ST	CAR	DRIVER	SPONSOR	LAPS
1	1	48	Jimmie Johnson	Lowe's Chevrolet	500
2	3	18	Kyle Busch	M&M's Halloween Toyota	500
3	15	5	Kasey Kahne	Hendrickcars.com Chevrolet	500
4	10	43	Aric Almirola	Gwaltney Ford	500
5	8	15	Clint Bowyer	5-hour Energy Avon Foundation for Women Toyota	500
6	32	2	Brad Keselowski	Miller Lite Dodge	500
7	11	24	Jeff Gordon	Pepsi MAX Chevrolet	500
8	2	55	Brian Vickers	MyClassicGarage.com Toyota	500
9	18	47	Bobby Labonte	Pine-Sol Toyota	500
10	30	16	Greg Biffle	3M Ford	500
11	17	39	Ryan Newman	Quicken Loans Chevrolet	500
12	9	27	Paul Menard	Zecol / Menards Chevrolet	500
13	27	22	Sam Hornish Jr	Shell Pennzoil Dodge	500
14	6	17	Matt Kenseth	Ford EcoBoost Ford	500
15	19	78	Kurt Busch	Furniture Row / Farm American Chevrolet	500
16	14	20	Joey Logano	The Home Depot / redbeacon.com Toyota	500
17	24	1	Jamie McMurray	McDonald's Chevrolet	500
18	23	99	Carl Edwards	Geek Squad Ford	500
19	34	83	Landon Cassill	Burger King / Dr Pepper Toyota	500
20	25	42	Juan Pablo Montoya	Target Chevrolet	500
21	20	88	Dale Earnhardt Jr	Diet Mtn. Dew/Nat'l Guard/AMP Energy Chev	500
22	4	31	Jeff Burton	Odyssey Battery / EnerSys Chevrolet	499
23	12	56	Martin Truex Jr	NAPA Auto Parts Toyota	499
24	33	9	Marcos Ambrose	Black & Decker Ford	499
25	22	13	Casey Mears	GEICO Ford	499
26	16	34	David Ragan	Where's Waldo? Ford	499
27	7	14	Tony Stewart	Office Depot / Mobil 1 Chevrolet	498
28	26	51	AJ Allmendinger	Phoenix Construction Chevrolet	498
29	28	32	Ken Schrader	Southern Pride Trucking / U.S. Chrome Ford	495
30	35	38	David Gilliland	Long John Silver's Ford	494
31	41	93	Travis Kvapil	Burger King / Dr Pepper Toyota	492
32	13	29	Kevin Harvick	Rheem Chasing the Cure Chevrolet	473
33	5	11	Denny Hamlin	FedEx Express Toyota	466
34	42	33	Stephen Leicht*	LittleJoesAutos.com Chevrolet	253
35	37	36	Dave Blaney	MOHAWK Northeast / TMone Call Center Chevrolet	193
36	29	10	David Reutimann	@TMone Drive Sales Fast Chevrolet	185
37	43	95	Scott Speed	Jordan Truck Sales Ford	116
38	31	26	Josh Wise*	MDS Transport Ford	85
39	21	98	Michael McDowell	Phil Parsons Racing Ford	61
40	40	30	David Stremme	Inception Motorsports Toyota	46
41	38	87	Joe Nemechek	AM/FM Energy Wood & Pellet Stoves Toyota	35
42	36	23	Scott Riggs	North Texas Pipe Chevrolet	22
43	39	91	Reed Sorenson	Plinker Tactical Chevrolet	19

*Sunoco Rookie of the Year Contender

NASCAR Sprint Cup Series TOP 12
(After 33 Races)

Pos.	Driver	Points	Pos.	Driver	Points
1	JIMMIE JOHNSON	2,291	7	MARTIN TRUEX JR	2,228
2	BRAD KESELOWSKI	2,289	8	MATT KENSETH	2,226
3	CLINT BOWYER	2,265	9	GREG BIFFLE	2,222
4	KASEY KAHNE	2,262	10	TONY STEWART	2,220
5	DENNY HAMLIN	2,242	11	KEVIN HARVICK	2,203
6	JEFF GORDON	2,237	12	DALE EARNHARDT JR	2,151

Previous spread: Speed and concentration are the watchwords as Matt Kenseth's team (No. 17) executes a pit stop at Martinsville Speedway. Behind them, Martin Truex Jr. (No. 56) and other drivers head down pit road and back to the track.

Opposite page: Tony Stewart is all business in the driver's seat of his Chevrolet.

Opposite page inset: The field creeps down Martinsville's frontstretch seconds before a restart.

Above: With his fist raised after his crucial victory in the heat of the Chase for the NASCAR Sprint Cup, race winner Jimmie Johnson exudes confidence and determination in Victory Lane at Martinsville Speedway.

34

AAA TEXAS 500

Forty-three drivers started the AAA Texas 500, many of them with a chance to put the winner's cowboy hat on their head after 334 laps around the 1.5-mile Texas Motor Speedway. But as the race wore on, and a perfect Texas day gave way to night, the two drivers in the forefront of the Chase for the NASCAR Sprint Cup – Jimmie Johnson and Brad Keselowski – were the two drivers fighting to win the race.

It came down to the final two restarts, which was one too many for Keselowski but just the right number for Johnson, who took a whipping in the first and dished one out in the second.

Johnson streaked under the checkered flag in his Hendrick Motorsports No. 48 Lowe's Chevrolet 0.808 of a second ahead of Keselowski to win his second Chase race in a row, which gave him a seven-point edge in the championship with only two races left. More significantly perhaps, it filled the five-time champion's tank to the brim with momentum. All year long, Johnson had used consistency more than dominating victories to stay in the hunt. Now, with the whole season on the line, he was winning again, albeit with Keselowski nipping at his back bumper.

Leave it to the 2011 NASCAR Sprint Cup champion, Tony Stewart, to sum it up, "What a battle this championship is."

Kyle Busch finished third, followed by Matt Kenseth and Stewart. Clint Bowyer finished sixth, doggedly holding onto his slim chance to become the Chase spoiler with a miracle comeback. He went to 2012's penultimate race at Phoenix International Raceway trailing Johnson by 36 points. Johnson led the most laps – 168 – which meant he was in front more than half the race. It was his fifth win of 2012 and the 60th of his career.

Under a yellow halo of sign poles, the entire field hits pit road at Texas Motor Speedway during the AAA Texas 500.

Nine yellow flags flew, including four in the final 60 laps, but it was the final two that made the difference. As Johnson put it: ". . . the gloves are off and it's bare-knuckle fighting. That second-to-last restart was pretty sketchy a couple of times how close we were and how hard we were racing. Luckily we brought the cars back, another caution came out and I got a great restart and got by him. We knew that we had the speed if I could just get by him."

When Johnson said "sketchy," he meant on Keselowski's part, because the young Penske Racing driver worked the five-time champ over pretty good while successfully staying in first, which is where he was when the green flag fell on that second-to-last restart.

It was Keselowski's race to win at that point, but with just four laps to go, Mark Martin and Carl Edwards crashed on the frontstretch, setting on a green-white-checkered overtime finish with one extra lap added to the race.

Johnson started to the outside of Keselowski, and this time he aggressively kept the younger driver pinned to the bottom of the groove. That gave Keselowski only two options: lift off the gas or slide up into Johnson and probably wreck them both. He lifted. He lost the lead, and the race.

"Yeah, I felt like we were just going to wreck," Keselowski said about lifting. "I wasn't looking to be the guy that wrecked him poorly. That's just not the way you want to run a race, and not the way I want to win a championship.

"I think the restarts made the difference," Keselowski said. "Jimmie probably would have gotten me with an extended amount of laps to go. But with only five or six to go when we had the lead, I felt pretty good about it. But getting that last yellow. . . I felt like

restarts are like rock, paper, scissors. Eventually you're going to lose them. It's just a matter of time. To win two out of three, I felt lucky to do that. Obviously, I didn't win the last one that counts."

Said Johnson, "I was two points (ahead) and now we've got seven. But there is a lot of racing left. We are running up front, running one-two all the time, (but) it doesn't mean it will be that way for the final two races."

34 | AAA Texas 500

FIN	ST	CAR	DRIVER	SPONSOR	LAPS
1	1	48	Jimmie Johnson	Lowe's Chevrolet	335
2	8	2	Brad Keselowski	Miller Lite Dodge	335
3	3	18	Kyle Busch	Snickers Toyota	335
4	10	17	Matt Kenseth	Ford EcoBoost Ford	335
5	21	14	Tony Stewart	Office Depot/Mobil 1 Chevrolet	335
6	4	15	Clint Bowyer	5-hour Energy Toyota	335
7	19	88	Dale Earnhardt Jr	National Guard/Diet Mountain Dew Chevrolet	335
8	18	78	Kurt Busch	Furniture Row Chevrolet	335
9	23	29	Kevin Harvick	Rheem/Budweiser Chevrolet	335
10	2	16	Greg Biffle	3M Ford	335
11	6	20	Joey Logano	Home Depot/redbeacon.com Toyota	335
12	36	39	Ryan Newman	Quicken Loans Chevrolet	335
13	5	56	Martin Truex Jr	Carlyle Tools by NAPA Toyota	335
14	16	24	Jeff Gordon	Drive to End Hunger Chevrolet	335
15	14	43	Aric Almirola	Farmland Ford	335
16	9	99	Carl Edwards	Aflac Ford	335
17	17	22	Sam Hornish Jr	Shell Pennzoil Dodge	335
18	24	1	Jamie McMurray	McDonald's Chevrolet	335
19	22	31	Jeff Burton	Caterpillar Chevrolet	335
20	12	11	Denny Hamlin	FedEx Office Toyota	335
21	20	13	Casey Mears	GEICO Ford	335
22	7	21	Trevor Bayne	Motorcraft/Quick Lane Tire & Auto Center Ford	335
23	38	93	Travis Kvapil	Dr. Pepper Toyota	335
24	32	10	Danica Patrick	GoDaddy.com Chevrolet	335
25	13	5	Kasey Kahne	Hendrickcars.com/Great Clips Chevrolet	334
26	41	83	Landon Cassill	Burger King Toyota	333
27	27	27	Paul Menard	Quaker State/Menards Chevrolet	332
28	33	34	David Ragan	CertainTeed/31-W Ford	331
29	11	55	Mark Martin	Aaron's Dream Machine Toyota	329
30	31	95	Scott Speed	B&D Electrical/TWD Ford	328
31	42	32	Ken Schrader	Federated Auto Parts Ford	328
32	15	9	Marcos Ambrose	Mac Tools Ford	310
33	29	47	Bobby Labonte	Wounded Warrior Project Toyota	284
34	25	42	Juan Pablo Montoya	Huggies Chevrolet	279
35	30	38	David Gilliland	Long John Silver's Ford	225
36	26	51	AJ Allmendinger	Phoenix Construction Chevrolet	107
37	35	26	Josh Wise*	MDS Transport Ford	41
38	37	98	Michael McDowell	Phil Parsons Racing Ford	37
39	40	36	Dave Blaney	Tommy Baldwin Racing Chevrolet	37
40	43	87	Joe Nemechek	AM/FM Energy Wood & Pellet Stoves Toyota	33
41	34	19	Mike Bliss	Plinker Tactical/MCM Elegante Toyota	32
42	28	37	J.J. Yeley	MaxQWorkForce.com Chevrolet	10
43	39	91	Reed Sorenson	Plinker Tactical/MCM Elegante Toyota	6

*Sunoco Rookie of the Year Contender

NASCAR Sprint Cup Series **TOP 12** (After 34 Races)

Pos.	Driver	Points	Pos.	Driver	Points
1	JIMMIE JOHNSON	2,339	7	DENNY HAMLIN	2,266
2	BRAD KESELOWSKI	2,332	8	TONY STEWART	2,259
3	CLINT BOWYER	2,303	9	MARTIN TRUEX JR	2,259
4	KASEY KAHNE	2,281	10	GREG BIFFLE	2,256
5	MATT KENSETH	2,267	11	KEVIN HARVICK	2,238
6	JEFF GORDON	2,267	12	DALE EARNHARDT JR	2,188

Previous spread: Pole winner Jimmie Johnson (No. 48) leads the field to the green flag to start the race, which he would ultimately win.

Opposite page inset: Joey Logano peers through his full-face helmet while seated in his No. 20 Home Depot/redbeacon.com Toyota.

Opposite page bottom: A windshield tear-off flies through the air as the gas man takes the second can of Sunoco fuel during a pit stop for Kevin Harvick's No. 29 Rheem/Budweiser Chevrolet.

Above: In Victory Lane at Texas Motor Speedway, Jimmie Johnson celebrates his second straight victory in the Chase for the NASCAR Sprint Cup and his fifth win of 2012.

35

Phoenix International Raceway
Sunday, November 11, 2012

ADVOCARE 500

Tires and tempers alike exploded in the AdvoCare 500 in the wildest race of an already exciting NASCAR Sprint Cup Series season, turning the Chase for the NASCAR Sprint Cup upside down for five-time champ Jimmie Johnson while giving a much-needed race win to Kevin Harvick.

While Harvick was celebrating in Victory Lane for the first time in more than a year, Jeff Gordon and Clint Bowyer were visiting the NASCAR transporter to discuss Gordon's deliberate and dramatic wrecking of Bowyer with barely a lap to go, which triggered a wild melee in the garage area as the fans in the front grandstand roared with the excitement of it all.

Meanwhile, Johnson and his team were loading up a wrecked race car and picking up the pieces after the seemingly bulletproof five-time champion hit the wall, both literally and figuratively, after his right front tire blew on lap 234 of the scheduled 312-lap event. He finished 32nd and fell 20 points behind Brad Keselowski, who scraped and clawed to a sixth-place finish, taking a shot in the side of his car about one second before he crossed the finish line, barely escaping an even-worse fate as a wild last-lap wreck erupted around him during a green-white-checkered overtime finish after seven extra circuits on the one-mile oval.

With Johnson's world turned upside-down, Keselowski left Phoenix to face down the season's final race at Homestead Miami Speedway with an unexpected 20-point cushion in NASCAR Sprint Cup Series points. All he would need to do was finish in 15th place or better and no matter how well Johnson ran, the Penske Racing driver would win his first championship, as well as a first NASCAR car owner championship for Penske.

"You always want to be in the lead of the points, especially in the closing races, so I'm thankful for that," Keselowski said.

Jimmie Johnson's No. 48 Lowe's/Kobalt Tools Chevrolet scrapes back across the track at Phoenix International Raceway after pounding the wall when a right front tire blew on lap 235, ending his chances in the race and putting him in a deep hole in his hopes for a sixth NASCAR Sprint Cup Series championship.

"But I also know that the troubles that they had are the same troubles that we could have next week, and so you try not to take anything for granted. You try to just focus on what lies ahead, and we've got to do the best job we can at Homestead. That's where my focus is."

Said Johnson, "It's way, way out of our control after the problem we had today. We still have to go to Homestead and race, and anything can happen down there. But [we're] not in the position you want to be in leaving Phoenix. But that's racing, and we'll go to Homestead and do all we can down there and see how things pan out."

Harvick won by keeping his uncommonly fast car near the front during the race while Kyle Busch dominated, leading 237 laps. But Harvick managed to outduel Busch on the final two restarts, starting from the outside row in his Richard Childress Racing No. 29 Budweiser Chevrolet. He won by 0.58 of a second over Denny Hamlin, with Busch in third, Kasey Kahne fourth and Ryan Newman fifth, though his car was demolished in the multi-car accident on the final lap.

"It was an interesting day to say the least, but [crew chief] Gil [Martin] did a great job of keeping us in the track-position game and made our car better all day, and the further we got towards the front, the better the car handled," Harvick said. "They made good adjustments, and there at the end we had a couple restarts and Kyle chose the bottom and we were able to drive around the top side of him and then get control of the race, really."

But the most searing memory from this race would be the sight of Gordon wrecking Bowyer, an act so rash he also took

himself out, as well as Joey Logano, with Aric Almirola involved as well. Moments earlier, Bowyer had slightly collided with Gordon, but the contact cut Gordon's tire, causing him to slide into the wall. Gordon continued as the race stayed green, but slowed and laid in wait for Bowyer to come back around before he pounced.

After Gordon emerged from his car in the garage, one of Bowyer's crewmen came at him, and a wild melee of mostly pushing and shoving broke out between the two crews and lasted for about 30 seconds as Gordon was held back and led away. Moments later, Bowyer came out of his wrecked car and made a mad dash down pit road, through the garage area and straight to Gordon's transporter, where a lone NASCAR official standing in front of the door managed to stop Bowyer's furious charge. There was more jostling as he was held back, but it soon settled into a simmer.

"Clint has run into me numerous times, wrecked me, and he got into me on the back straightaway and pretty much ruined our day," Gordon said. "I've had it, fed up with it and I got him back."

"When you're disrupting a championship run like that, it's too bad," said Bowyer. "They asked us not to do that in the driver's meeting and there's usually a lot of respect there. Like I said, it's crazy – I didn't even need to pass him. I was plenty content riding behind him and he slipped up down there, I get under him and here he comes back. I just barely touched him. I literally barely rubbed him and then all the sudden I feel him trying to retaliate."

Bowyer dropped to fourth in NASCAR Sprint Cup points, 52 points behind, with no chance of winning. With 35 races down and one to go, only Johnson and Keselowski were still in it.

35 | AdvoCare 500

FIN	ST	CAR	DRIVER	SPONSOR	LAPS
1	19	29	Kevin Harvick	Budweiser Chevrolet	319
2	3	11	Denny Hamlin	FedEx Ground Toyota	319
3	1	18	Kyle Busch	M&M's Toyota	319
4	4	5	Kasey Kahne	Farmers Insurance Chevrolet	319
5	12	39	Ryan Newman	Quicken Loans / U.S. Army Chevrolet	319
6	14	2	Brad Keselowski	Miller Lite Dodge	319
7	20	16	Greg Biffle	Filtrete Ford	319
8	6	78	Kurt Busch	Furniture Row / Farm American Chevrolet	319
9	7	27	Paul Menard	Rheem / Menards Chevrolet	319
10	10	55	Mark Martin	Aaron's Dream Machine Toyota	319
11	13	99	Carl Edwards	Fastenal Ford	319
12	21	42	Juan Pablo Montoya	Target Chevrolet	319
13	33	31	Jeff Burton	Caterpillar Chevrolet	319
14	22	17	Matt Kenseth	Ford EcoBoost Ford	319
15	30	47	Bobby Labonte	Vektor Vodka Toyota	319
16	5	43	Aric Almirola	Farmland Ford	319
17	37	10	Danica Patrick	GoDaddy Racing Chevrolet	318
18	17	9	Marcos Ambrose	Black & Decker Ford	318
19	9	14	Tony Stewart	MOBIL 1 / Office Depot Chevrolet	318
20	39	93	Travis Kvapil	Burger King / Dr Pepper Toyota	318
21	23	88	Dale Earnhardt Jr	Diet Mtn. Dew/AMP Energy/Nat'l Guard Chevrolet	317
22	25	13	Casey Mears	GEICO Ford	317
23	18	1	Jamie McMurray	Bass Pro Shops / Allstate Chevrolet	317
24	8	51	Regan Smith	Phoenix Construction Chevrolet	316
25	27	83	Landon Cassill	Burger King / Dr Pepper Toyota	316
26	42	36	Dave Blaney	Accell Construction Chevrolet	316
27	15	20	Joey Logano	Dollar General Toyota	312
28	16	15	Clint Bowyer	5-hour Energy Toyota	312
29	41	32	Timmy Hill	U.S. Chrome / TMone Ford	312
30	11	24	Jeff Gordon	DuPont Chevrolet	309
31	26	22	Sam Hornish Jr	Shell Pennzoil Dodge	299
32	24	48	Jimmie Johnson	Lowe's / Kobalt Tools Chevrolet	281
33	29	34	David Ragan	Barrett Jackson Ford	280
34	32	30	David Stremme	Inception Motorsports Toyota	86
35	35	33	Stephen Leicht*	LittleJoesAutos.com Chevrolet	74
36	31	38	David Gilliland	Loan Mart Ford	50
37	38	26	Josh Wise*	MDS Transport Ford	50
38	28	98	Michael McDowell	Phil Parson Racing Ford	36
39	43	87	Joe Nemechek	AM/FM Energy Stoves/aloft hotel tempe Toyota	30
40	34	44	David Reutimann	No Label Ford	28
41	36	19	Mike Bliss	Plinker Tactical / Value Place Toyota	15
42	40	91	Jason Leffler	Plinker Tactical / Value Place Chevrolet	10
43	2	56	Martin Truex Jr	NAPA Auto Parts Toyota	10

*Sunoco Rookie of the Year Contender

NASCAR Sprint Cup Series TOP 12
(After 35 Races)

Pos.	Driver	Points	Pos.	Driver	Points
1	BRAD KESELOWSKI	2,371	7	GREG BIFFLE	2,293
2	JIMMIE JOHNSON	2,351	8	KEVIN HARVICK	2,285
3	KASEY KAHNE	2,321	9	TONY STEWART	2,284
4	CLINT BOWYER	2,319	10	JEFF GORDON	2,281
5	DENNY HAMLIN	2,309	11	MARTIN TRUEX JR	2,260
6	MATT KENSETH	2,297	12	DALE EARNHARDT JR	2,211

Previous spread: As Kevin Harvick (No. 29) crosses the finish line to win the AdvoCare 500, Ryan Newman spins toward a fifth-place finish in the first milliseconds of the multi-car accident that occurred as the field pounded toward the checkered flag.

Opposite page: Clint Bowyer's crew pushes his battered No. 15 5-hour Energy Toyota back to the garage after he was wrecked by a revenge-seeking, soon-to-be-penalized Jeff Gordon with only a lap to go in the regularly scheduled race. It sent Bowyer reeling to a 28th-place finish and ended his run as a contender in the Chase for the NASCAR Sprint Cup.

Above: Kevin Harvick hoists the winner's trophy in Victory Lane at Phoenix after posting his first victory of the 2012 season.

36

Homestead-Miami Speedway
Sunday, November 18, 2012

FORD ECOBOOST 400

As Brad Keselowski proved yet again that the last miles in the Chase for the NASCAR Sprint Cup are the hardest, Jeff Gordon showed what a difference a week can make by winning the Ford EcoBoost 400 in a nail-biting finale at Homestead-Miami Speedway.

Keselowski, who needed to finish only 15th or better to win his first NASCAR Sprint Cup championship, was in real danger of losing the title without really messing anything up all that badly, battling as he was against a brilliant pit strategy by challenger Jimmie Johnson that put the five-time champion on a path toward Victory Lane.

But with 62 laps to go, Johnson's team stumbled on what would have been his last pit stop and gave it all away. The rear tire changer missed tightening a lug nut on the left rear wheel and NASCAR ordered Johnson back to the pits to fix it, costing him a lap and any chance at the championship. As if to cement his doom, Johnson's Chevy broke 20 laps later with a rear gear failure and sent him to the garage and a 36th-place finish.

Keselowski, meanwhile, managed to claw his way back to the 15th-place finish he had to have to win the title no matter what, which meant a lot to him. "We were not as fast as we wanted to be, I'll be the first to admit that, but my guys never gave up, we kept working and at the end we were capable of getting back up enough to where it wouldn't have mattered if he had won, which made me feel a lot better," Keselowski said.

The third-year driver gave team owner Roger Penske his first NASCAR Sprint Cup car owner's championship after 40 years in the sport, the last 21 as a full-time owner. "The goal I've had for all of my racing career is to be at the top of this sport," Penske said.

Early in the race, Brad Keselowski (No. 2) was dogged by Jimmie Johnson (No. 48) as he battled for his first NASCAR Sprint Cup Series championship. But the contest was destined to get a lot tougher for the young Michigan driver before it got easier.

And for the second week in a row, the old veteran Gordon found a way to hog some of the spotlight for himself in his Hendrick Motorsports No. 24 DuPont 20 Years Celebratory Chevrolet. At Phoenix International Raceway at the end of the season's penultimate race, Gordon purposely and spectacularly wrecked Clint Bowyer in retaliation for cutting his tire and putting him into the wall a few laps earlier. NASCAR fined Gordon $100,000 and 25 points for the rash move, but did not suspend him for the season's final event, a break that he made the most of by winning the race. He did it with the same plan Johnson had – save enough gas to make one less pit stop than the others.

Gordon took the checkered flag 1.028 seconds ahead of Clint Bowyer, who was followed by Ryan Newman, Kyle Busch and Greg Biffle. Bowyer followed the same gas-saving plan as Gordon, and his runner-up finish allowed him to move past Johnson for second in the championship. Johnson's DNF left him 36th in the race.

"I knew we had a great race car going into the race and, you know, at times I didn't think we had a winning car," Gordon said. "But you know what, we played the strategy perfectly and had a really good car and, you know, it's just unbelievable to experience this." It was his 87th career victory and his second of 2012, but,

surprisingly, it was not only his first win at Homestead, but the first win there for car owner Rick Hendrick.

Bowyer, too, experienced far happier feelings at Homestead after the bitter taste of Phoenix. "I didn't see that coming," he said of overtaking Johnson for second in the Chase for the NASCAR Sprint Cup. "I had no idea. I didn't even think we could reach second."

Kyle Busch dominated the race, leading 191 of the 267 laps, but he was foiled in the end by the gas-saving strategy of Gordon and Bowyer and had to make a stop for a splash of Sunoco fuel with just a few laps to go.

"This is the way you want to win a race," Gordon said, "by just going to battle with them and having a good race car and playing it all out really smart. Having my family in Victory Lane means more to me than anything. It's something that (during) those 13-win seasons and all those things, I didn't have. So, this is just an amazing feeling to get my first win at Homestead as well as Rick Hendrick's first win at Homestead. And to do it with this 20th Anniversary DuPont car, especially after what happened last weekend, is incredible. I didn't think we'd be able to get to Victory Lane this weekend."

36 | Ford EcoBoost 400

FIN	ST	CAR	DRIVER	SPONSOR	LAPS
1	15	24	Jeff Gordon	DuPont 20 Years Celebratory Chevrolet	267
2	6	15	Clint Bowyer	5-hour Energy Toyota	267
3	19	39	Ryan Newman	U.S. ARMY Chevrolet	267
4	8	18	Kyle Busch	M&M's Toyota	267
5	13	16	Greg Biffle	3M/SP Richards Ford	267
6	7	56	Martin Truex Jr	NAPA Auto Parts Toyota	267
7	5	43	Aric Almirola	Smithfield Ford	267
8	23	29	Kevin Harvick	Budweiser Chevrolet	267
9	26	78	Kurt Busch	Furniture Row Chevrolet	267
10	16	88	Dale Earnhardt Jr	National Guard/Diet Mountain Dew Chevrolet	267
11	18	27	Paul Menard	Menards/Duracell Chevrolet	267
12	4	99	Carl Edwards	Fastenal Ford	267
13	2	9	Marcos Ambrose	Black & Decker Ford	267
14	1	20	Joey Logano	Home Depot/redbeacon.com Toyota	267
15	3	2	Brad Keselowski	Miller Lite Dodge	266
16	9	55	Mark Martin	Aaron's Dream Machine Toyota	266
17	35	14	Tony Stewart	Office Depot/Mobil 1 Chevrolet	266
18	11	17	Matt Kenseth	Best Buy Ford	266
19	33	31	Jeff Burton	Caterpillar Chevrolet	266
20	14	1	Jamie McMurray	Bass Pro Shops/Tracker Boats Chevrolet	266
21	12	5	Kasey Kahne	Farmers Insurance Chevrolet	266
22	17	22	Sam Hornish Jr	Shell Pennzoil Dodge	266
23	20	21	Trevor Bayne	Motorcraft/Quick Lane Tire & Auto Center Ford	266
24	41	11	Denny Hamlin	FedEx Express Toyota	266
25	32	47	Bobby Labonte	Clorox Toyota	265
26	38	93	Travis Kvapil	Dr. Pepper Toyota	265
27	30	83	Landon Cassill	Burger King Toyota	265
28	21	42	Juan Pablo Montoya	Target Chevrolet	264
29	28	13	Casey Mears	GEICO Ford	264
30	24	51	Regan Smith	Phoenix Construction Chevrolet	264
31	34	34	David Ragan	Ford	263
32	31	36	Dave Blaney	Florida Lottery Chevrolet	263
33	40	38	David Gilliland	Long John Silver's Ford	262
34	37	10	David Reutimann	TMone in Iowa City, IA/Spearfish Chevrolet	261
35	39	37	J.J. Yeley	C&C Audio Video & Appliance, Inc. Chevrolet	261
36	10	48	Jimmie Johnson	Lowe's Chevrolet	224
37	42	32	Ken Schrader	Federated Auto Parts Ford	219
38	22	30	David Stremme	Swan Racing Toyota	183
39	27	6	Ricky Stenhouse Jr	Fifth Third Ford	157
40	36	26	Josh Wise*	MDS Transport Ford	38
41	25	98	Michael McDowell	Phil Parsons Racing Ford	34
42	43	23	Scott Riggs	North Texas Pipe Chevrolet	23
43	29	19	Mike Bliss	Plinker Tactical Toyota	16

*Sunoco Rookie of the Year Contender

NASCAR Sprint Cup Series TOP 12
(After 36 Races)

Pos.	Driver	Points	Pos.	Driver	Points
1	BRAD KESELOWSKI	2,400	7	MATT KENSETH	2,324
2	CLINT BOWYER	2,361	8	KEVIN HARVICK	2,321
3	JIMMIE JOHNSON	2,360	9	TONY STEWART	2,311
4	KASEY KAHNE	2,345	10	JEFF GORDON	2,303
5	GREG BIFFLE	2,332	11	MARTIN TRUEX JR	2,299
6	DENNY HAMLIN	2,329	12	DALE EARNHARDT JR	2,245

Previous Spread: With his first championship finally in hand, Brad Keselowski (No. 2) celebrates with race winner Jeff Gordon (No. 24) as they do simultaneous burnouts on the frontstretch at Homestead-Miami Speedway.

Oppsite page: A dejected Chad Knaus, crew chief for Jimmie Johnson's No. 48 Lowe's Chevrolet team, walks in front of his crippled Chevrolet as it sits on jack stands in the garage while the crew tries to repair the broken rear gear that put him out of the race.

Above: An ebullient Jeff Gordon sprays the champagne in Victory Lane after winning the season finale at Homestead-Miami Speedway, his second victory of the 2012 season.

REFLECTIONS 2012

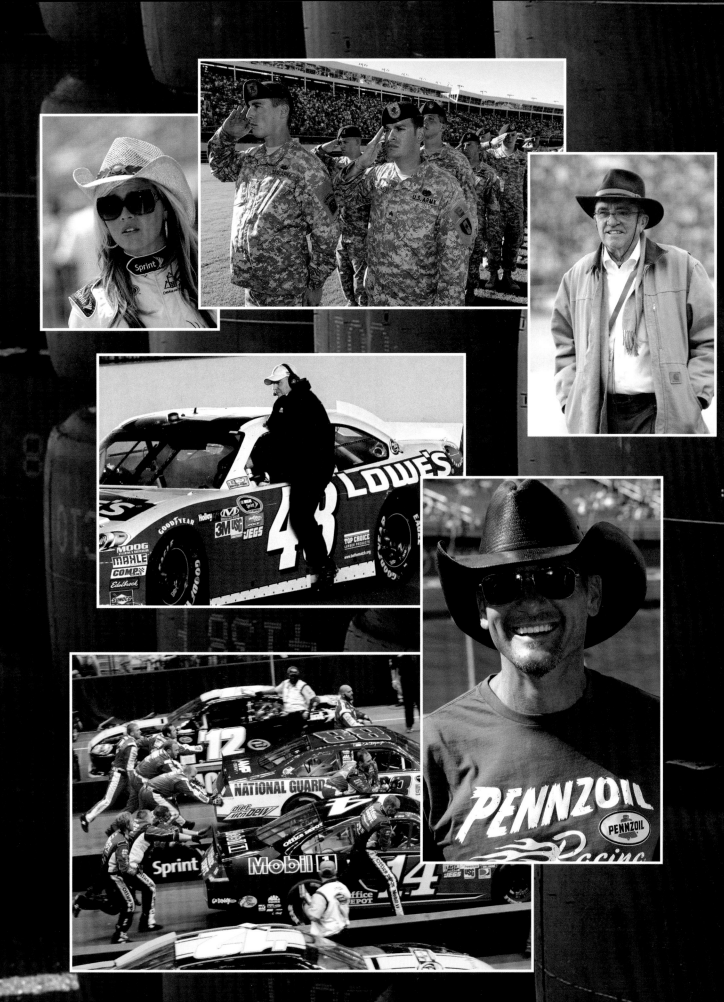

AUTOGRAPHS

The NASCAR Sprint Cup Series
Yearbook 2012